HERE
ON THE WAY TO
THERE
A CATHOLIC PERSPECTIVE ON DYING AND WHAT FOLLOWS

WILLIAM H. SHANNON

ST. ANTHONY MESSENGER PRESS
Cincinnati, Ohio

Cover design by Constance M. Wolfer
Interior pages by Mark Sullivan

LIBRARY OF CONGRESS CATALOGING-IN-PUBLICATION DATA

Shannon, William Henry, 1917-
Here on the way to there : a Catholic perspective on dying and what follows / William H. Shannon.
   p. cm.
Includes bibliographical references and index.
ISBN 0-86716-596-0 (alk. paper)
   1. Death—Religious aspects—Catholic Church. 2. Future life—Religious aspects—Catholic Church. 3. Terminal care—Religious aspects—Catholic Church. 4. Catholic Church—Doctrines. I. Title.

BT825.S53 2005
236'.1—dc22

                                        2004024676

ISBN-13: 978-0-86716-596-8
ISBN-10: 0-86716-596-0

Published by St. Anthony Messenger Press
28 W. Liberty St.
Cincinnati, OH 45202
www.AmericanCatholic.org

Printed on acid-free paper.

Printed in the U.S.A.

06 07 08 5 4 3 2

❧ Contents ❧

❧ Introduction ☙

Not long after I chose the title of this book, *Here on the Way to There,* I enjoyed dinner at a Chinese restaurant. At the end of the meal, the waiter gave me the customary fortune cookie. I opened it and it read: "You are almost there." I was startled for a moment. It fit so aptly with my title. I wondered, "Will I have time to finish writing this book?" Then I began to reflect that, in the light of our total existence, that very clear message is true of every one of us. We *are,* all of us, "almost there"—some closer than others. We all need to live with this thought, not in any morbid way, but honestly facing our future—never knowing how close we are to being "almost there," and finally to being "there."

This is written for those who are "here, but almost there," which really means all of us mortals. I hope to discuss some of these questions: How does "life here" relate to "life there"? How does "life here" prepare us for "life there"? How can we help those who are imminently close to "there" ready themselves for the big transition? How do we ready ourselves for that same experience? And, finally, there is the really big question: What can we say about "life there"? What is it like?

HERE

DYING, DEATH AND ENTERING INTO NEW LIFE

One way of judging what a society believes about the meaning of life is to look at the way it deals with death.

Death happens to the best of us; actually to all of us—sooner or later. C.S. Lewis once wrote to a correspondent: "There is nothing discreditable in dying. I've known the most respectable people to do it." Lewis's remark reminds me of a delightful story that came out of a catechist's experience. The catechist had been teaching the children about grace and salvation. To make sure they understood the importance of God's grace, she asked them a number of questions. First she asked, "If I sold my house and my car and had a big garage sale and gave all my money to church, would that get me into heaven?" "No," they answered. "If I cleaned the church and mowed the lawn and made everything neat and tidy, would that get me into heaven?" Again their answer was, "No." "If I was kind to animals and gave lots of candy to children, would that get me into heaven?" Once again they replied, "No." Then, expecting them to display what they had learned about grace and salvation, she asked them, "Well, then, how can I get into heaven?" One five-year-old boy shouted out, "You gotta be dead!"

Now that I have (hopefully) gotten your attention, let me offer my credentials for writing a book on death and what follows. Obviously I have not experienced death personally, but I have experienced it vicariously—and many times. As chaplain at the motherhouse of a congregation of religious women, I see death quite regularly. Living in a community of mostly elderly nuns (the oldest being full of years at ninety-eight, with quite a few not far behind), it is not surprising that we have a rather large number of deaths each year. We are quite conscious of what Emily Dickinson called "death's tremendous nearness." We accept "Sister Death" as a respected member of our community.

I find it interesting that people who come here for a wake or a funeral are invariably surprised, even puzzled, to find that the overriding emotion they experience here is not sadness, but joy. We rejoice in and celebrate a life fulfilled. A sister whom we love and who died in our midst is now alive with the fullness of God. The card that goes out to announce her death reads: "Sister _____ entered into eternal life on _____, 2006." Her death becomes a community celebration: an expression of our Christian faith that glories in the belief that God's love for us extends far beyond the grave into eternity. God's grace conducts our loved ones through death's portal to new life. I do not mean to suggest that we are uncaring or that we don't feel a sense of loss. Oftentimes there are tears, but at the very heart of those tears is the calming joy of knowing that a life has achieved its fulfillment, that someone we love is in the embrace of divine love.

I once said in a homily at the funeral Mass of one of our sisters:

> Dying in this house is a *holy moment*, as you experience a person (whether conscious or not) making her final act of freedom, saying her ultimate yes to God. It is a *holy moment* because one who dies here is always surrounded in those dying moments by people who care, people who love, and people who pray. It is a *holy moment* because the more than nine hundred sisters who have already said their final yes to God in years gone by are also in that room praying and readying a joyous welcome for the new arrival.

Many people, I suspect, are mystified by the way faith-filled Christians look upon and speak about death. In fact, it is probably true to say that not a few Christians themselves are confused and unclear about what their faith has to say about this universal human phenomenon. For, let's face it, we live in a cultural context that inevitably exercises its influence on us; there is probably no area of human life in which Christian faith is more out of step with American secular culture than in its approach to death. Our American secular culture is uncomfortable with death, even embarrassed by it. It is something no one wants to talk about—at least not directly. It seems easier—and less unpleasant—to say "John passed away." It is almost as if there were something obscene about simply saying, "John died." Woody Allen, in his impish way, expressed this discomfort with death when he said: "I'm not afraid to die; I just don't want to be there when it happens." The reason for this lack of ease with death is that so many people see death as only loss, and the loss is total. Death is the final diminishment: the end of life and all the good things that life had meant. Death is cruel: the final irreversible tragedy in human affairs.

The *American Heritage Dictionary* may be taken as a fairly accurate embodiment of American secular culture. It defines the noun "death" as the "termination of life," and the verb "to die" it describes as "to stop living." Christian faith, on the other hand, would describe the noun "death" as "the beginning of life—life at its best, at its most real," and the verb "to die," it would define as "to start living in a different and most wondrous way." It would be hard to find a sharper contrast than the difference between these two statements about death. And the difference is crucial. For the way people view death determines, or at least contributes to, the way they live before death. The one truly perspective-giving question that everyone has to face is this: "Does death terminate everything, or does death begin something—something far greater than we have ever known or can ever know in this life?"

This book is written to make clear that the Christian choice is the second alternative: Death begins something new and wonderful. This choice makes sense, not because we have experienced death, but because we have the certainty of faith. Faith gives us a language and a vocabulary that enable us to talk about what we have not yet experienced. It is a language that takes its source from the one human being who has overcome death not just for himself but for all of us. Jesus dead and risen is the epicenter of

Christian faith. "Epicenter," the focal point of an earth-quake, is a useful way of describing the earth-shaking event of the Resurrection of Jesus. The Resurrection set human history on a whole new course. Lancelot Andrewes, a seventeenth-century Anglican writer, expressed it simply and starkly: "So mortal He was, when He ours; but now when we His, He is immortal, and we brethren to Him in that state, the state of immortality."[1]

An Important Distinction: Dying and Death

All right, you may want to say, I hear what you are saying: "Faith tells us that death may bring something new and wonderful." But what about death itself? You're not suggesting that there is something wonderful about death, are you? When I see someone whom I love dying, gasping for breath, writhing in pain, I fail to see anything wonderful about that. All I can see is something distressful and demeaning. How can you speak in praise of death, which brings such suffering to people?

Let me try to respond by suggesting that there is a way of understanding death that, in an altogether unique way, sees it as *freedom in action*. What does this mean? To understand and embrace this way of viewing death we need to distinguish two different experiences: (1) the experience of death and (2) the experience of the process that precedes it, namely, dying.

The Process of Dying

There is a passivity about dying: It is passive in the sense that it happens *to* us. I am reminded of the story of the salesman staying in a motel in the South who ordered breakfast and noticed something on his plate that he did not recognize. He asked the waitress what it was. She said, "Them's grits." "But I didn't order them," he said. She answered, "Oh, you don't order grits. They just comes." That's the way with death: It just comes. We don't choose it. It is beyond our control. Generally, there is no way of predicting when it will come and whether it will be a relatively easy process or an excruciatingly painful one. We have no way of knowing whether or not it will be a long, drawn-out process or something that happens quickly, suddenly and unexpectedly.

We all know of cases where death seems to come easily and without very much suffering. That was true, I know, in my mother's case. The process of her dying was quick and, as far as we could grasp, without pain. One morning my father called me and said, "Your mother is asleep, and I cannot wake her up." Her dying was difficult for me and especially for my father, but for her it was probably quite painless as she slept her way into the arms of a loving God. Apparently it was much the same for a close friend of mine who died recently. He had terminal cancer. He knew it. The day before he died, I visited him. He seemed quite comfortable. We chatted about the many common interests we had shared. Eventually, we got to talk about his impending death. Finally we got to talk about the process of dying that he was going through. His last words to me were: "If this is what dying is like, it's not so bad."

Yes, I think it is true that there are cases when dying happens easily and without too much discomfort. In how many cases this is true, I do not know. But I suspect the number is relatively small. In most cases dying is a process that can be painful and unpleasant. It is not easy to die. We have to wait until it happens. The process of dying, therefore, may be described as a *passion*. I use the word "passion" not in the ordinary dictionary sense of "a strong emotion" or "a sexual desire," but in its etymological sense. Linguistically *passus* is the past participle of the Latin word *pati*, which means "to suffer," "to endure." It is in this sense that we speak of the *Passion* of Jesus. It was something that others did to him, something he endured. It involved the horrible pain that accompanies so barbarous a death experience as crucifixion. Over the centuries Christian people have meditated on the sufferings of Jesus and the love for humankind, which those sufferings so clearly expressed. Our reflection on the passion of Jesus helps us to endure the sufferings that life brings to us, especially that final suffering of dying.

Dying, therefore, must be viewed as a process that is part of the human condition. No one can escape it. It is the sword of Damocles suspended over all of us. "Damoclean sword" is a fitting image to describe the precariousness of human existence and the inevitability of the dying process that sooner or later we must all succumb to. According to Greek legend, Damocles, a courtier in the court of the tyrant ruler of Syracuse, had to sit at a banquet table under a sword suspended over him by a single thread. No one escapes the severing of that thread.

I am sure all of us know of cases when dying seems to bring cruel, unbearable suffering for people we love. So often we feel helpless to do anything that would lessen their pain. The best we can do is to suffer with them. This is what *com*passion means: to suffer with someone else, especially someone we love. In the last several decades, compassion has taken on a new name: It is called hospice care.

The hospice movement has revolutionized our understanding of and our approach to the dying process, whether we talk about our own dying or that of someone we love. *While we have no control over the fact that we shall die, hospice care makes it possible for us to control the way we die.* Hospice is about giving care and comfort that will enable a terminally ill person to die with dignity and in peace. Two basic goals identify the hospice movement: (1) people who are dying have the right to decide how they will spend their remaining days, and (2) they have the right to spend their remaining days as peacefully and comfortably as possible.[2]

It would be quite wrong, therefore, to think that the dying process is *purely* passive as if nothing active were going on in the person during that process. As a matter of fact much may be going on in the dying person. Here we touch on mystery. Things are happening in the dying person that oftentimes are at a level of consciousness that family, caregivers, friends simply cannot reach. There is a gradual detachment from the outside world and a moving inward. The person is moving toward the freedom that comes with death. Doctors and nurses may be able to alleviate, and hospice personnel would insist, even eliminate physical suffering. But there are other kinds of suffering that may dog the minds and hearts of the terminally ill. There are still issues of the spirit that must be dealt with, unfinished business that needs to be worked through. It is a time of letting go: letting go not only of wonderful relationships that brought joy, but also relationships that call for regret and reconciliation. A dying person who has been juridically absolved through the sacrament of reconciliation from evil actions done in the past may still be troubled by a kind of existential guilt: the sense not just of having *done* something wrong, but also of *being* wrong. The person may need the time to forgive himself or herself and open the depths of his or her heart to God's forgiving love.

Here is a concrete story illustrating what I mean. A man in his seventies was admitted to hospice care. Palliative care helped reduce his pain so that within a few days, he was free from pain. Yet from the moment he entered hospice, his face bore a look of anguish that he seemed unable to let go of. His family made clear that he had not lived a good moral life. There was a shady side to his life. There were many regrets he had to deal with. Clearly there was a painfulness of spirit that he still had to come to grips with. One day, with the anguished look still fixed on his face, he said to his family: "I am not ready yet." Eight days passed. No one seemed able to get through to him. Something seemed to be holding him back. Finally one afternoon his wife and sons went into his room. They knew immediately that something had happened within him. His countenance was changed from anguish to peace and calm. Not long afterward he died in the arms of his hospice nurse. In a way no one could understand or explain, he had worked through what it was that had brought such anguish to his face and gained peace and calm as he died into the arms of a loving God.[3] He was saying, "Now I am ready. There is nothing holding me back." He was no longer resisting the dying process. In a sense he was giving that process permission to move toward its ultimate conclusion, that is, into the action of death.

Another (more pleasant) story concerns an aunt of mine. I was pretty much her only caregiver. When she was no longer able to remain in her apartment, I arranged for her to enter St. Anne's Home in Rochester, New York. On one of my regular visits to her, I noticed that someone (I never found out who) had placed on the dresser in her room a photo of herself. It was an elegant picture of a young woman beautifully dressed including a fur around her neck and a flapper's cap on her head. The photo was a gift to her father and across it she had written "Happy Birthday, Dad 1930." I had the photo framed and managed to get it hanged on the wall where she could easily see it. Each time I came to visit her, I asked her, "Who is that beautiful woman?" Her answer was always, "I don't know." When I insisted it was her picture, she simply denied it. This same conversation went on for a number of visits. Then one day, soon before her death, I put the question again: "Who is that beautiful woman?" A big smile came over her face and she said, "That's me." It was such a surprise to me! I could only feel that a new sense of freedom and the beginning of the experience of new life had entered into her consciousness from the depths of her being. In one way she was already beginning to experience the meaningfulness of death.

Another instance of a similar experience was told to me by Diane Branch, a Sister of St. Joseph. On Thanksgiving Day, 1978, she told me:

> My brother and I visited our mother in a nursing home. She hadn't much energy but sat in her chair listening to news about the family. All of a sudden in the midst of our conversation, she rose from her chair and started

with sure step toward the door. My brother asked, "Where are you going, Mom?" She looked back at us as if we should understand, "I have to go home now," she said. That evening I returned and tucked her into bed with, "I'll see you tomorrow." At 11 PM I received a call telling me that she had slipped away not long after I had left. Now the words "I have to go home now" are very precious to me and have comforted me all these years.

Experiences of this sort are often referred to as "nearing death awareness."

Nearing Death Awareness

This "nearing death awareness" happens more than we realize. Sometimes dying people who seem disoriented may say things or make gestures that seem to make no sense. It is helpful to realize that they may be operating at a level of consciousness not open to us. Caregivers need to listen in order to decipher the meaning of the messages they are attempting to convey. It is well to take notes on what they say. They may be talking about what they are experiencing but cannot express at the level of ordinary consciousness. They may be asking for someone they need to see in order to have a peaceful death. The experience of dying not infrequently provides glimpses of another world, even of loved ones waiting the dying person's arrival.

A number of people who read the first printing of this book have told me stories of such experiences. Sister Denis told me about the time she was called to St. Mary's Hospital to be with her brother whose death was imminent. She arrived at his bedside just before he died. She stood close to him with her hands on his arm. All at once he sat up by himself and reached out his hand as though to someone beckoning him to come. There was a beautiful smile on his face. Then, he fell back on his pillow and breathed his last.

Elisabeth Kübler-Ross

It is appropriate at this point to mention a person who, as much as anyone, helped move people to a more positive approach to the process of dying. Elisabeth Kübler-Ross was a psychiatrist and author of the groundbreaking book *On Death and Dying* (1969). This book raised the awareness of the whole world to a wholesome way to view the natural phenomenon of death. It was her healthy approach to viewing dying that has become the basic philosophy behind the hospice movement. She named and described the five psychological stages of the dying process: denial, anger, bargaining, depression and, finally, acceptance. Patients, families and caregivers often go through these stages, though, it is important to note, that they do not necessarily occur in any particular order. People may fluctuate among the various stages throughout the dying process. What these stages involve is really the human search for meaning: "Why am I going through this experience? Why don't I understand God's plan for me? Is there a God, and if there is, why so much suffering?" Doctors, nurses and caregivers need to listen to patients and allow them, even encourage them, to express their feelings. Silent presence and listening to the patient's feelings and beliefs may be more healing than trying to answer their questions. Dr.

Kübler-Ross's approach to the dying process will be considered in more detail later in part two of this book.

Death

Death, I want to maintain, is something quite different from dying. Whereas dying is a passion and a process, something that happens to us (though not without some involvement on our part and on the part of our caregivers), *death is preeminently something that we do.* It is, therefore, an *action.* The most important action in all our lives. At the moment of death, in a way that bystanders cannot see, a person stands before God, stands face to face with divine Goodness, divine Beauty and says "yes" to God. Death is a moment of absolute clarity and complete freedom. In the divine presence, all the things that might distract us in this life are gone. We shed them as a serpent sheds its skin. All through life we strive to say "yes" to God and to God's will for us. That "yes" is sometimes firm, sometimes hesitant. At death there is no longer anything to lure us into false affirmations, nothing to prevent us from speaking out a resounding, joyful, wholehearted "yes" to God.

Death is not the end of a contest wherein prizes and penalties are handed out to winners and losers. It is going home to the only home that will satisfy our deepest hopes and yearnings.

Death as Seeing the Face of God

In Psalm 42 the psalmist cries out, "My soul thirsts for God, / for the living God. / When shall I come and behold / the face of God?" The psalmist is expressing a desire we all have whether we ever articulate it or not. Yet in our mortal existence, there is a veil that, as it were, hides the face of God from our vision. It may be compared to something that happens to most of us as we grow older. We acquire cataracts that place a veil over our eyes and obscure the clarity of our vision. People who have had cataract surgery know how different one's vision becomes after that surgery: Colors become ever so more vivid; one is able to read numbers in the telephone book without a magnifying glass! Death may be viewed as a kind of spiritual cataract surgery. It gives us new vision: that wondrous vision which we call beatific (happiness-producing). In death we see the face of God.

Death as Seeing Our Own Faces

But there is more. In the act of death I say "yes" not only to God, but also to myself, to the true self that all through life I have been struggling to become. It's a struggle because in this life our energies are scattered. We are never fully ourselves. In the act of death we at last attain to the fullness of who we are. We become who we are—and forever. In death we at last cease to live the illusion of a separate, self-centered existence and realize that our life is—and always has been—lived with God in Christ and with our sisters and brothers.

To put this another way: Death not only enables us to see the face of God, it also makes it possible for us to see our own faces. Did you ever stop to think that you cannot see your own face? And your eyes—which are sometimes called the windows of the soul—can't be seen either. You see with your eyes. But you cannot see your eyes. You might want to say: "But I can see my face and I can see my eyes, when I look into a mirror." Ah, but it is not your eyes that you see in the mirror; it is the reflection of them. It is not your face that you see in the mirror, but the reflection of your face. The reflection of your face is not your face.

This inability to see our own face is a kind of metaphor that tells us that, as we travel through life, we do not really know ourselves. Our face is the most expressive part of our physical being: it registers our thoughts, our feelings and our emotions. It is our face that makes us vividly present to others. It is something outward that tells us something of what is inside, something visible that helps us to see something of what is invisible.

Suppose you were to walk into a room and see twenty people—each without a face. To put it mildly, it would be an eerie, unsettling experience. You would be seeing a group of "nobodies." To think of a person without a face is to imagine someone with no personal identity.

The Unrepeatable Uniqueness of Each and Every Person

A person's face, then, is a symbol of that person's identity. Therefore, when I say that we cannot see our own faces, I am really saying that we cannot know our own identity. We cannot know what makes us unique. We can talk about the many qualities and gifts of character that so beautifully emerged in the lives of various people. Yet I dare say that there is no one who is able to put into words the personal uniqueness of any one individual, say, a parent, a spouse, a child and a friend. Vladimir Lossky has written what I think is a very perceptive insight about the limitations of every attempt to describe an individual person. He says that, when we wish to define or characterize a person, we gather together certain traits of character, but these are never uniquely personal, because they are characteristics that are also possessed in varying degrees by other persons. "We admit," he says, "that what is most dear to us in someone, what makes him himself, remains indefinable, for there is nothing in nature which properly pertains to the person, which is always unique and incomparable."[4] Hence, try as we will, we cannot capture in our words that which makes a person the unique reality that he or she is. That reality is unrepeatable.

Not only can we not define her uniqueness, but she herself, while in our midst, could not put words to that uniqueness. It remained a mystery to her, perhaps even more of a mystery to her than it was to us. It is a mystery known only to God. To put this into metaphorical language, she could not see her own face. Only God could see her face. For her as for others it was veiled and hidden from view.

Death is the unveiling of that mystery. All through our mortal life we struggle with the question, "Who am I?" At various times we get certain insights into the answer, but never quite capture the answer in its fullness. Our whole life story is our effort to affirm the unique person we really are. It is our vain effort to see our own face. But never in this mortal life are we able to see our own face. Never are we able to make a full affirmation of that which makes us uniquely who we are.

The wonderful thing about the experience of death is that every person has the opportunity to make this affirmation and to make it in a final and definitive way, not *before* death, not *after* death, but *in* death, that is, at the moment of death. All through the mortal phase of our existence before death, the "yes" we say to our unique self, like the "yes" we say to God, is always partial and incomplete. At the moment of death we are set free to make the choice we want to make, but as yet cannot. Robert Nowell has written,

> At the moment of death the human person is set free
> from all the limitations which in this life cloud our deci-
> sions, and is thus able to make the kind of choice toward
> which we aspire, but which [in this life] we are never
> [quite] able to achieve.... Our decisions in this life are
> necessarily made on the basis of partial knowledge....
> But if death represents our final and definitive en-
> counter with God, then it means encounter with the full
> light of truth, and thus with the ability at least to decide
> in full knowledge of what is involved.[5]

To put it another way, death is the final and decisive "sacrament" of our encounter with the risen Jesus, as he strives to make us into himself. It is only in the sacrament of death that Jesus' task of remaking us is fully complete, as we surrender our total being to his transforming touch. Death is thus the sacrament of total absorption into God; yet it is an experience that is uniquely personal to each one of us. We become fully in God what we have been striving to become all our lives (even if we didn't know that that was what we were striving for). We become in God the totally unique persons that each one of us is. It is a uniqueness that is unrepeatable in any other person. In death I get to know at last the "I" that heretofore was known only to God. I at last awaken to who I really am. In death I get to see my own face.

Thus it is that in death we achieve the complete answer to the prayer Saint Augustine puts on our lips: *"Noverim te, noverim me."* (May I know you, may I know myself.)

It is clear, then, that death and dying represent two different experiences; still we need to look at them in terms of continuity and discontinuity. There is continuity between dying and death because *our existence continues after death.* There is discontinuity, because *our existence after death is radically different from our existence before death.* Before death, our existence is mortal; after death it is immortal. Let me explain.

Existence: Mortal and Immortal

None of us will ever forget the terrible act of terrorism of September 11 that demolished the World Trade Center.

Life is eternal; and love is immortal; and death is only a horizon; and a horizon is nothing save the limit of our sight.[6]

Nor can we ever remove from our imaginations the heart-rending photos that we witnessed of women and men, at that scene of fearful destruction, standing on the street holding up a picture of a loved one and pleading with anyone who went by: "Have you seen this person? This is my husband, my daughter, my son. Please tell me: Have you seen him? Have you seen her?" The voices were voices of pure anguish that bordered on despair—the terrible feeling that their loved ones were gone. A heinous act of terror had taken the lives of this dear relative or friend. It was a terrible experience for them to face the fact that their loved ones had died and they would never see them again.

Some months ago I celebrated Mass for a classmate and dear friend who had gone to God. As I was preparing the Missal, I turned to the section called "Masses for the Dead." I had opened the Missal to that section many times before. But on this occasion, something happened to me. It suddenly occurred to me that I was bothered by this title in a way that I never had been before. There was something theologically questionable about it. I knew that my friend had died and gone to God (something about which I could only rejoice) but equally I knew that his dying was a brief experience that led to new and glorious life. *I could not think of my friend as dead.* I could only think of him as alive—alive in a much fuller sense than I am alive or that you the reader are alive.

When God created my friend, God gave him an eternal existence. Part of that existence was mortal: the life he lived on earth. That phase of his existence ended with his death. But death, which ended his mortal existence, ushered in the beginning of the immortal phase of his existence: his life in God. Death was a momentary experience between these two phases of his existence. He has moved, through death, to that immortal life that was the purpose for which he was created. Beyond the trials and problems of this mortal life, he now lives a life that is eternal, as God's life is eternal. I wanted to rejoice in his achievement of life's goal. That is why I experienced the wrongness of using a "Prayer for the Dead" for someone who was so very much alive.

Jacques Maritain, a well-known and highly respected twentieth-century Catholic philosopher, in an article in *Jesus Caritas* expressed the same feeling that I was experiencing:

There is something that I find scandalizing about the way Christians speak of their deceased. They call them the dead—they haven't shown themselves capable of renewing the miserable human vocabulary on a point which nevertheless touches the essential tenets of their faith. The dead! One attends masses for "the dead"! One goes to the cemetery with flowers for "the dead"! One prays for "the dead"! As if they weren't milliards of times more alive than we! And as if the fundamental truth stated in the Preface of the Burial Mass: "vita mutatur, non tollitur"—"life is changed, it is not taken away"—were itself a dead truth, incapable of fecundating and transforming the too general routine of our manner of thinking and speaking.[7]

As Maritain suggests, we need to watch our language when we speak about the essential tenets of our faith; and at the heart of our faith is the truth that human existence is eternal, but in two stages. The experience of death is just a "blip," so to speak, between mortality and immortality, on the trajectory of human existence. Why then should that blip, that moment—"death"— determine the language we use to describe those who have passed into new life? So instead of prayers for my friend as dead, I want to pray for him and with him and to him as a person who is alive and immortal in the wondrous communion of saints! Wouldn't it be a joy to see the Missal prayers "for the Dead" changed to a more correct and appropriate title that would make clear that we are talking about the (very much alive) communion of saints? It would be not only joy, but also a far better theology, a better way of expressing the *total picture of human life*, as only faith can grasp it.

But What About Those Who Are "Left Behind"?[8]

I realize that what I have said does, in the context of our Christian faith, make sense when we are speaking of the person who has died. As the French playwright Jan Anouilh has said, "Death is beautiful. It alone gives love its true home."[9] But the situation is very different for those who have experienced the loss of a loved one. To lose a parent or a spouse or a child or a dear friend leaves a void and an emptiness in a person's life that nothing and no one else can fill. Only time and a strong sense of God's love can assuage, in part at least, the grief and heartache that death inevitably brings to those who are "left behind." This is a situation (and I hope to discuss it at greater length later in this book) where Christian community can prove a source of strength and hope for those who mourn. There is also need on the part of the bereaved to confront the deepest problems about life's meaning and its transcendent purpose. Many readers will perhaps remember the poignant story of C.S. Lewis in the movie *Shadowlands* wherein a professor, who had lectured learnedly about all sorts of topics in a speculative way, suddenly is called upon to face the very practical issue of the death of Joy, the woman he had come to love so passionately. In his grief he seems inconsolable. There is one moving scene, in which his adopted son says to him: "Jack, do you believe in heaven?" After a brief pause, he answers: "Yes, I do." The distraught youngster says: "Well, I don't." In the days following, the man and the boy take many quiet walks together. Finally, Lewis says to the boy: "We live only in the shadow lands. Your mother lives the only life that is truly real and full of joy." John Milton uses the same image:

> What if Earth
> Be but the shadow of Heav'n, and things therein
> Each to other like, more than on earth is thought?[10]

Saint Aloysius, a sixteenth-century Jesuit who died at the age of twenty-three, wrote a tender letter to his mother from his deathbed. He begged her to rejoice that he was soon going to God:

> Take care above all things, most honored lady, not to insult God's boundless loving kindness; you would certainly be doing this if you mourned as dead one living face to face with God, one whose prayers can bring you in your troubles more powerful aid than they ever could on earth. [He assures her:] Our parting will not be for long; we shall see each other again in heaven; we shall be united with our Savior; there we shall praise him with heart and soul, sing of his mercies forever, and enjoy eternal happiness.[11]

Immortal, Eternal Life

In death the human person attains his or her definitive state. But immortal, eternal life does not mean that things go on as usual, as if we were simply moving to a new page in our personal story, with life continuing as it was before we died. Eternity is not just a lot more time given to us. I can recall as a young altar boy being fascinated by my pastor's description of eternity (and, as I recall, he usually spoke of it in connection with hell). He would create this mind-boggling picture: "Suppose," he used to say, "a bird would come once every thousand years and drop one grain of sand in this building. By the time that this building would be full and overflowing with sand, eternity would scarcely have begun."[12] I always thought it a great image and eagerly anticipated the time he would use it again—and sure enough he did. The problem is that it is very bad theology. Far from being a lot of time, eternity actually takes us out of time and releases us from the limitations time imposes on us in our mortal existence.

Resurrection, Not Resuscitation

To put this another way, life after death is resurrection, not resuscitation. That is why the prototype of our immortal existence is not Lazarus (who died and was *resuscitated*) but Jesus (who died and was *raised to new life*). Think of the Lazarus story in the fourth Gospel. The raising of Lazarus meant that he was restored to life, but to the same life he had lived before his death. It would seem reasonable to expect that he returned to life at the same age as he had been when he died. Thus, his resuscitation would have meant that his life was prolonged for some years or even some decades, depending on how old he was when he died. Still the time would come when, like all mortals, he would have to die once more. Perhaps as he grew older and feebler in this resuscitated life, he would have let go of any desire to be resuscitated again. His dying wish to the executor of his will may well have been: put a DNR (do not resuscitate) sign beside my grave. And don't let Jesus get near it!

What happens to us in death is not mere resuscitation, but resurrection. The prototype of our resurrection is the Resurrection of Jesus. Saint Paul speaks of Jesus as the first-born from the dead. Thus, in Colossians: "He is the head of the body, the church; he is the beginning, the firstborn from the dead, so that he might come to have first place in everything" (1:18). The same thing is said in Romans: "For those whom he foreknew he also predestined to be con-formed to the image of his Son, in order that he might be the firstborn within a large family" (8:29).

Now, if you read the post-resurrection stories in the Gospels, you see so clearly that Jesus' life after Resurrec-tion was new: It was totally different from the life he had lived for more than three decades among his family, friends and followers. That is the intriguing puzzle that the resurrection stories make evident to us. Clearly, after the Resurrection, he was the same Jesus they had known and followed: They recognized his voice, they touched him. They shared meals with him. The Gospels very definitely emphasize the physical character of his appearances. (To use a term I employed earlier: There was *continuity* between the mortal Jesus and the risen Jesus.)

The Gospels make equally clear that there was some-thing bewilderingly different about the risen Jesus. He was no longer subject to the limitations that mortality places upon us (and indeed placed on him, too, before his Resurrection). Once risen, he could be present to his friends, without their recognizing him. He could enter rooms where the doors were shut. He could appear suddenly and just as suddenly disappear, as he did with the two disciples with whom he broke bread at Emmaus. Clearly there was *discontinuity* between the Jesus of history and the risen Jesus who transcends time and space.

The New Creation

The life of the risen Jesus was indeed a new creation, immeasurable by time, because it was not a "coming back" from the dead. It was a going beyond death. It was not a coming back to mortal existence (as was true for Lazarus). It was entrance into the life of God. The Risen One—the man of Galilee who had lived among people—can never die again. He is totally in God who is all life. Jesus entered into an entirely new kind of existence: an immortal existence that robbed the grave of its victim, not temporarily, but forever.

Before the Resurrection of Jesus, the whole world was seen as a graveyard. From Adam to Jesus, the destiny of everyone born into this world was the grave. The human story was: birth, life, death and corruption in the grave. Period. True, people dreamed about a life after the grave. The Pharisees of Jesus' time believed in the resurrection of the body. They hoped for it, longed for it.

And there were Greek philosophers, like Plato, who looked forward, not to resurrection of the body (to him that would have been disaster), but to the survival of souls. He thought of death as a separation of body and soul, which brought liberation to a soul that had been imprisoned in a body.

Yes, before Jesus all that people knew for sure was that every man, woman and child would end up in the grave. Thomas Gray's "Elegy in a Country Churchyard" has put mournful words to this most cruel human fate:

> The boast of heraldry, the pomp of power,
> And all that beauty, all that wealth e'er gave,
> Await alike th' inevitable hour:
> The paths of glory lead but to the grave.

Jesus' Resurrection gave a new message to humanity. The human story is no longer: birth, life, death and corruption. It has become birth, life, death and life everlasting. The message of the Resurrection (Jesus' Resurrection, that is, and our resurrection that will be) is that the human body matters. These beat-up bodies that we are—with our bad hearts, our weak eyesight, our poor hearing, our arthritic joints and all the other maladies we carry around—are going to be transformed. They're going to be glorified. For Christ has risen! And because Christ has risen and because he is the firstborn of many brothers and sisters, nothing can ever be the same for humanity again. Nothing can ever be the same for the universe. As Paul says: "For this perishable body must put on imperishability, and this mortal body must put on immortality" (1 Corinthians 15:53). Or hear also Paul to the Romans: "If the Spirit of him who raised Jesus from the dead dwells in you, he who raised Christ from the dead will give life to your mortal bodies also through his Spirit that dwells in you" (8:11).

It was God's love that raised Jesus from the dead. God's love would not let him perish. And it is God's love that will not let us perish, that will enable us to live forever. "Men and women can no longer totally perish, because they are known and loved by God. All love wants eternity, and God's love not only wants it but effects it."[13]

Our conviction that we shall not perish, but will live forever, is based on our belief in the trustworthiness of God. John Polkinghorne in an article in the (London) *Tablet* wrote:

> Appeal to that belief was exactly the way in which Jesus countered the disbelief of the Sadducees (Mk 12:18-27). He reminded them that God was the God of Abraham, Isaac, and Jacob. The patriarchs mattered to God once and so they must matter to God for ever. Israel's God is "God, not of the dead, but of the living." If we matter to God now, as we certainly do, then we shall matter to God for ever. At death we shall not be cast aside like broken pots on some cosmic rubbish heap. Human beings are not naturally immortal, but the faithful God will give us a destiny beyond our deaths.[14]

It should be clear that, when we speak of the "resurrection of the body" in the Creed, we are not talking about our present condition of life being prolonged—even prolonged indefinitely, even prolonged forever. No, when we speak of "the resurrection of the body and life everlasting" we are talking about a life that is new, completely different from our present mortal existence. Yet it is still we—the persons we really are—who enter into this new life, this immortal, eternal life.

Eternal Life and Nondualism

One point I need to emphasize: We are talking about eternal life for persons, not just for souls. The biblical understanding of eternal life is radically different from that of the Greek philosophers. The Greek philosophers saw personal survival in terms of a *soul* that was immortal. In Plato's *Phaedo*, Socrates, who is facing imminent death, discourses eloquently on immortality, just before drinking his hemlock "cocktail." As he explains it, people are composite beings, made up of two elements, alien to one another: an immaterial soul and a material body. The soul had a prior existence, but somehow has gotten attached to a material body. To Plato (as I have pointed out earlier) mortal existence meant an imprisonment of the soul in a material body—an imprisonment that restricted its freedom. For him, therefore, death was the great liberator, for it freed the soul from the encumbrances of the body. With death the soul was free to return to its proper habitat: the world of ideas where Truth, Goodness and Beauty are eternal.

This dualism—that sees the human person as composed of two divisible, even alien, elements—has continued to influence Christian thought. Remember the *Baltimore Catechism* question: "Of which should we take greater care: our soul or our body?" The answer of course was: "we should take greater care of our soul, for it is destined to live forever with God in heaven." Yet another instance of this dualism is the fact that we continue to pray for the *soul* of John Smith instead of for John Smith the person.

Our Christian tradition, it seems, has never quite recovered from the overdose of Platonic philosophy that it swallowed very early. Yet this dualistic understanding of the human person is bad theology. It is in conflict with the biblical understanding of the human person. Christian belief is that death brings about a transfiguration of the whole human being. The soul cannot exist without a body. Therefore, after death human beings do not cease to be embodied persons. It is I, the person, who survives death, not just my soul. To put it another way: My soul is not I. I am more than my soul. I am the relationships I have established, the history I have lived, the consciousness I have experienced—all this as an embodied person. *What is at stake in the resurrection of the body, therefore, is not the continuity of the body simply as a physical entity, but the continuity of the person.* All that makes this person to be this person continues to exist. Personal immortality in an "embodied" form is what we mean by the Christian belief in the "resurrection of the body."

Again, Jesus is the prototype. As I have already mentioned, Saint Paul speaks of Jesus as the firstborn from the dead. His life after Resurrection was radically new: totally different from the mortal life he had lived in Palestine for more than three decades. Yet after the Resurrection, he was the same Jesus his followers had known. Even his wounds, now no longer sources of pain, but symbols of his victory, are visible to them. It was the same Jesus, but he was different: no longer subject to the limitations that mortal life had placed on him.

If Jesus is the firstborn of many brothers and sisters, then our risen life will resemble his. We shall be persons, marked with our own unique individuality. Like Jesus we shall enter into the very life of God as embodied persons.

Some people may have difficulty thinking that those who go to God have a body (or better, are a body) that is new, yet the person is the same person.

Even from a scientific point of view, what we call the body is an ever-changing constellation of atoms, none of which persist throughout a mortal life. Resurrection of the body does not mean the survival of a matrix of particular atoms, but identity and continuity of persons and lives in a process of final transformation.[15]

When you think of your parents or grandparents or relatives and friends who have gone to God, do you think of them as asleep or do you think of them as the persons you remember?

In the creed we express our belief in "the resurrection of the body and life everlasting." It seems to make sense to say that both "the resurrection of the body" and "life everlasting" are experienced at the end of each person's mortal existence, which for that person is *the end of time.* This would seem to preclude an interim period between death and final resurrection, when souls will be asleep waiting the final judgment day *at the end of time.* For to think in this way of our loved ones who have died would mean that the very ancient tradition of praying to the saints would have no real meaning. It is surely the sense of the faithful that they can address as living persons those who have died. Indeed this is part of our devotion to the saints—a devotion that we express so meaningfully in the litany of the saints.

Recently a friend of mine told me that he had gone to Chicago to visit his mother who was dying. She asked him,

"Michael, what's going to happen to me when I die?" His answer was, "I don't know, Mom, but I know it's going to be much better than it is now." I chided him a bit, by saying, "Mike, you can do better than that. Don't you realize that you are the same person you were ten years ago; yet, because the body cells change every seven years, you, while remaining the same person, are not the same body at all? That is what we mean when in the creed we express our faith in the resurrection of the flesh, the resurrection of the body. Death is a transformation of the whole being, the person. What is at stake, therefore, is not the continuity of the body as a physical entity (which, as I mentioned, changes every seven years or so) but the continuity of the person. All that makes this person to be this person continues to exist. Do figure out a way of telling this to your mother. In risen life she will be herself, the person she has always been, yet wondrously transformed in the image of Jesus."

Wouldn't it be neat to think that our risen bodies also change every seven years? Except, of course, seven years are terms of time, and death moves us out of time. Surely one of the joys of heaven will be that we continue to grow as persons. But I need to stop at this point, for I am already intruding into a later part of this book that will be explicitly about heaven.

In the light of what has been said above, what do you think of the following prayer that is frequently said at funerals or wakes?

Eternal rest grant unto her, O Lord;
and let perpetual light shine upon her.

May she rest in peace.
May her soul and the souls of all the faithful departed
through the mercy of God rest in peace.

Note the contrast in the prayer between her (the person)
and her soul. Would it be more correct to say in the last
part of the prayer: "May she and all the faithful departed
through the mercy of God rest in peace"?

Catholic Funeral Rites

All through our lives liturgical rituals play an important
role. We celebrate in ritual what we can never express fully
in words. When deeply experienced, ritual moves us into a
level of consciousness that we do not ordinarily experience. We touch upon the mystery of our relation with the
transcendent. "Ritual action is especially important at
times of greatest mystery, for events we find difficult to
apprehend because they are too beautiful or too sorrow-
ful."[16] Three different rites comprise the Catholic Funeral
Liturgy: (1) the Vigil for the person who has gone to God,
(2) the funeral Mass, and (3) the Rite of Committal. The
movement in these rites from one place to another symbolizes the Christian's pilgrim journey from this mortal life
to God. The United States Conference of Catholic Bishops
expresses the important beliefs and values affirmed in the
Catholic Funeral Rites:

> ...the sacredness of all human life, the dignity of the
> individual person; the resurrection of Jesus Christ, the
> first born of the dead, and of his faithful followers;
> death as an occasion to confront and embrace human
> mortality; the respect that is to be shown to the bodies

of the dead and offering prayers for them; and the need of the Church to provide a ministry of consolation to those who mourn.[17]

What Does the Church Teach About Cremation?

When you visit a funeral parlor, what you see in the casket is no longer the body of your friend or family member who has died; it is a corpse. There is a difference between a body and a corpse. A body is a unity in which all its elements comprise a living unified whole; a corpse, on the other hand, is made up of various elements that with time will disintegrate and be reduced to its basic elements. It has, therefore, a unity that is only accidental. This disintegration will occur slowly but inevitably when buried; it will disintegrate quickly when the corpse is reduced to ashes by cremation.

What, then, is the meaning of the resurrection of the body? A passage in Augustine's *Confessions* is helpful. In Book IX Augustine tells of his conversation with his mother, Monica, just before she died. It was his desire to return her corpse to her native land (Africa). She, however, was unconcerned about where her remains would be laid. She said to him: "Lay this body [corpse] anywhere, let not the care of that disquiet you: this only I request that you would remember me at the Lord's altar wherever you be."[18] Note how she asks remembrance for herself the person, not just for her soul. This coincides with the sense of the faithful who, when they think of their beloved who have gone to God, express a clear belief that they are persons; they do not think of them as disembodied souls waiting years and eventually even centuries for bodily

existence. The Christian meaning of resurrection is, therefore, belief in the mystery—and it is a great mystery
indeed—that God gives our loved ones a continued bodily existence when they enter into eternal life. This is no
more mystery than the reality I have already spoken of,
whereby our living bodies so change over the course of
years that the body I now have is entirely different in its
basic composition than it was ten years ago, yet I am still
the same person. So when our beloved ones who are with
God enter into eternal life, it is God's graciousness that
makes them embodied persons.

It is in this context that the church's teaching on cremation can be understood. In the 1880s the church condemned the practice of cremation because it was "un-
Christian and Masonic in motivation." It was not cremation
itself, but the motives that prompted it that were condemned. For there is no essential difference between cremation and burial. Cremation by fire and heat does quickly
what burial does slowly but inevitably: it reduces the corpse
to ashes. In 1963 the prohibition of cremation was lifted,
and in the 1989 edition of the Order of Christian Funerals
there were included prayers for the committal of the cremated remains. In 1997 the American bishops were given
an indult by the Congregation for Divine Worship and the
Discipline of the Sacraments to allow the presence of the
cremated remains at a funeral Mass.

The revised *Code of Canon Law* makes clear that, while
permitting cremation where it is requested, the church
prefers burial. Thus, the *Code* says, "The Church earnestly
recommends that the pious custom of burying the bodies
of the dead be observed; it does not however, forbid cre-

mation unless it has been chosen for reasons that are contrary to Christian teaching."[19]

There are a number of reasons for preferring burial. Jesus was buried. Early Christians reverenced the burial places of the martyrs.

> This is the body once washed in baptism, anointed with the oil of salvation and fed with the bread of life. Our identity and self- consciousness as a human person are expressed in and through the body....[20] Thus the Church's reverence and care for the body grows out of reverence and concern for the person whom the Church now commends to the care of God.[21]

When cremation is chosen for a good reason, the full Order of the Christian Funeral is to be celebrated, including the Vigil Service, the Eucharist and the Rite of Committal. The question sometimes arises whether or not cremation may take place before the Vigil and funeral Mass. The church clearly prefers and urges that, if there is to be cremation, that it take place after the Rite of Final Commendation. The diocesan bishop, however, may for a good reason permit the cremated remains to be present for the liturgy, which should be done in its entirety.

The cremated remains must be given the same respect as the body, including the use of a worthy container for them and the way they are carried and transported. They should be buried or entombed in a cemetery. Scattering cremated remains or keeping them in the home do not fit the kind of reverence and respect due to the corporeal remains of a human person. In recent years the practice has developed in some parishes of constructing columbaria somewhere within the church where the cremated remains may be placed. Church law ordinarily forbids the burial of corpses in churches.

Should a person be considering cremation as the option he wishes to choose for his funeral, he would be wise to discuss this with family, parish priest and the Catholic Cemetery Office.

What Does the Church Teach About Organ and Tissue Donation?

Transplantation of donor organs and tissue is a miracle of modern medicine that is able to save the lives of the recipients of such donations. A single organ donor can save the lives of up to eight people by donating heart, lungs, liver, pancreas, kidneys and intestines. One tissue donor can improve the lives of fifty people by donating eyes, bone, soft tissue, heart valves, veins and skin.[22]

Organ and tissue donation is approved, even encouraged, by the church. Pope John Paul II, speaking of gestures of everyday heroism, said: "A particularly praiseworthy example of such gestures is the donation of organs, performed in an ethically acceptable manner, with a view to offering a chance of health and even life itself to the sick who sometimes have no other hope."[23]

The *Catechism of the Catholic Church* distinguishes organ transplants *(inter vivos)* and *postmortem* donations.

Organ transplants [inter vivos] are in conformity with the moral law if the physical and psychological dangers and risks to the donor are proportionate to the good that is sought for the recipient. Organ donation after death is a noble and meritorious act and is to be encouraged as an expression of generous solidarity.[24]

The *Catechism* goes on to make two cautionary statements. The first is that organ donation is not morally admissible if the donor or his or her proxy has not given explicit consent. The second declares organ transplants between living persons to be morally illicit, if it brings about disabling mutilation or death of the living donor.

One of the problems associated with organ donations after death is the need to be sure that the donor is dead. The *Ethical and Religious Directives for Catholic Health Care Services*, published by the USCCB, states: "Such organs should not be removed until it has been medically determined that the patient has died. In order to prevent any conflict of interest, the physician who determines death should not be a member of the transplant team."[25]

The determination of death is left to medical experts. In the past death was defined as the irreversible cessation of heart and respiration. Today the criterion accepted for certifying that one is dead is brain death. This occurs when there is total and irreversible cessation of all brain function, including the brain stem. The Pontifical Academy of Science has stated that death occurs when "there has been an irreversible cessation of all brain functions, even if cardiac and respiratory functions which would have ceased have been maintained artificially."

My Commitment to Donate Life
Uniform Donor Card

I, _____, have spoken to my family about organ and tissue donation. The following people have witnessed my commitment to be a donor. I wish to donate the following:

[ ] any needed organs and tissue
[ ] only the following organs and tissue:

_____

Donor signature _____date _____
Witness _____
Witness _____

Family Notification Form

Dear _____,
I would like to donate life by being an organ and tissue donor. I want you to know my decision because you will be consulted before donation can take place.
I wish to donate the following:

[ ] any needed organs and tissue
[ ] only the following organs and tissue:

_____

Thank you for honoring my commitment to donate life through organ and tissue donation.
Donor signature _____date _____

☙ PART TWO ❧

HERE ON THE WAY TO THERE

SOME REFLECTIONS ON GROWING OLDER

Grow old along with me!
The best is yet to be,
  the last of life, for which the first was made:
Our times are in His hand
Who saith: "A whole I planned,
Youth shows but half; trust God: see all nor be afraid."[26]

Growing older is a human phenomenon from which there is no escape. All of us, whatever our age, are each day growing older. The fifteen-year-old, desperately wanting to get that driver's lesson, is impatient to grow older. The eighty-year-old, on the other hand, is quite content to grow older at a different pace and for different goals.

There is no doubt that we live in a culture that glorifies youth and has little room for the aged. People resist getting old. A multibillion-dollar industry caters to the tastes of those who want to remain youthful-looking at all costs.

As I was reflecting on this phenomenon, I remembered an event from my past. It was a Saturday more than forty years or so ago. I went to Our Lady of Lourdes parish in Rochester to take part in a wedding Mass. Father Donald Cleary was also involved in the wedding. Before Mass he said to me, "Bill, I wish tomorrow would never come." Surprised, I asked him why. His answer was, "Because tomorrow I am going to be fifty years old." I suppose that, as I was in my thirties then, I felt sympathetic toward him as age was beginning to take its toll. Funny how my perspective has changed. Now I look back to fifty as the flowering of youth. But Don Cleary's fearfulness of growing old was symbolic of an attitude in our culture. In a culture that worships youth to the point of obsession, old age is simply not understood.

Indeed, people feel they are paying a compliment if they praise an elderly person for looking youthful. Would it maybe be much more appropriate and accurate to praise them for the dignity and beauty of their age? I recall meeting a middle-aged man, with whom I was but slightly acquainted. He said to me, "How are you, *young man*?" I am sure he did not expect my reaction. I said to him, "Joe, you know and I know that I am not a young man. There is a wisdom that comes with age and I would expect people to respect that."[27] I suspect he will be more circumspect about what he says to older people in the future. Thomas Merton has written: "There is a kind of foolish legend about old people, a legend by which the old are rendered acceptable because they retain some vestiges of youth. The foolish platitude that praises the old for being 'like kids' rather than for the dignity of their age." He goes on to say:

"It is certainly very fine for old people to be full of the vigor of youth, but they should not have to cling to that *alone* as a way of being acceptable to the rest of the world. On the contrary, their age has a wonderful quality which makes them worthy of special respect and love."[28] There is a sense of mystery and wonder about them, as they are—some more than others—on the last stages of a journey that will bring them to the threshold of eternity.

Do we tend—consciously or not—to treat the elderly as if they were children?

The Diminishments of Old Age

> When the signs of age begin to mark my body (and still more when they touch my mind); when the painful moment comes in which I suddenly awaken to the fact that I am ill or growing old...in all these dark moments, O God, grant that I may understand that it is you (provided only my faith is strong enough) who are painfully parting the fibers of my being in order to penetrate to the very marrow of my substance and bear me away within yourself.[29]

To be sure, old age is a time of diminishment: diminishment of one's circle of friends and of one's involvement in family and society, also the diminishment of mobility and of some of life's activities. It is a time of bereavement of letting go of activities that once were a normal part of one's life. Thus, visiting the local shopping plaza—formerly a brief part of a number of a day's activities—becomes the major achievement of the day. Actions like climbing stairs or a satisfactory trip to the bathroom—once done almost without thought—become major accomplishments. Giving up your driver's license, because you realize that your slower reflexes are no longer an adequate match for today's rapid traffic, can be an agonizing and traumatic experience. Old age is a time of letting go; happy are those who learn to do it graciously. And blessed are those who understand what is happening and continue to deal with the aged in a way that respects their dignity and maturity.

The Beatitudes of the Aged

Blessed are those who understand my slow steps and my shaking hands.

Blessed are those who notice that my ears have to strain to hear what they are saying.

Blessed are those who perceive that my eyes are clouded and my reactions are slow.

Blessed are those who look the other way when I dribble at the table.

Blessed are those who please me with a smile, giving me time to talk about things of no importance.

Blessed are those who never say, "You've told me that a thousand times!"

Blessed are those who know how to talk about what happened in the past.

Blessed are those who make me feel that I'm loved and not abandoned.

Blessed are those who understand how hard it is for me to carry my cross.

Blessed are those who help me make that last journey to the Promised Land, treating me with love and tender care.

The Best Is Yet To Be

"The best is yet to be
the last of life, for which the first was made…"

So wrote Robert Browning at the age of forty-nine. He died at seventy-seven. Did his thoughts on aging change over those last twenty-eight years? I hope not. I hope he remained upbeat as he went through the process of aging. Do you agree with Browning's words? It depends, I suppose, on your outlook—whether you are an optimist or a pessimist.

Four men met every morning for coffee. All four were pessimists. They spent their time together lamenting the bad news of all the evils that plagued the world, each one trying to top the others with even worse news. One day, to the surprise of the others, one said, "I have decided I am going to be an optimist." The next day when they gathered, one of the men said to him, "Patrick, did you really mean that you are now going to be an optimist?" He answered, "Yes, I *am* an optimist." "But," the others said to him, "You look so distraught and sad and anguished." He looked them all in the face and said, "You think it's easy to be an optimist these days?"

I must say that, even though it isn't always easy to be one, I am an incurable optimist. Living to a ripe old age (I think I qualify; I won't tell you my age, but my birth was the reason my father was not drafted in World War I) is truly, I believe, a wonderful gift. Not all appreciate this gift, though. It can be easy to get so caught up in the burdens and the diminishments of aging that it is hard to see the good things it brings.

A Worthwhile Question

If someone were to ask, "Do you like being old?" what would I say? Well, we optimists might say something like this: We like being old. It has set us free. We rather like the persons we've become. Of course, we have made our share of mistakes. But we've also done a lot of things that have brought us joy—joy that we have been to share with others. We are quite happy to be who we are right now. Our lives aren't as cluttered as they used to be.

But we optimists—now that we have let go of a lot of things that we once thought we had to do—have time to reflect, to evaluate our lives and to realize the store of wisdom we have been able to accumulate over the years. Moreover, it is important and healthy to realize that life's inevitable diminishments need not mean the cessation of continued meaningful growth in various, even unexpected areas of human life. Indeed, in significant areas of life, diminishments may become opportunities for growth. It is not just that one grows in spite of diminishments, but rather a person can in some ways grow precisely because of them.

By uncluttering our lives, "getting on in years" (as some people euphemistically describe old age) can give us what we are continually clamoring for during the earlier years of life: time—time for quiet and rest, time just to be, no longer feeling driven to define ourselves in terms of what we do.

For so many years we struggled (often unsuccessfully) to achieve some kind of equilibrium in our lives between the demands our activities impose on us on the one hand, and the deep human need for contemplation and reflection on the other. Age brings balance into our lives. We have a much better sense of what's worth doing and what isn't. Also, we are free to be kind to ourselves and less critical of who we are and what we ought to be doing. We no longer feel the need to prove ourselves to others or to ourselves. We know that we have succeeded in some measure in managing our lives. The seeming failures of the past no longer appear as catastrophic as they once did.

Then there is that wonderful gift of memory. Even though we can sometimes forget the name of our best friend, we have memories. Wonderful remembrances of family, friends and good times. True, there are some memories that we may have forgotten, or we may give a rosy color to experiences that in their happening were not so joyous (but maybe that may actually be seeing them in better perspective). And, yes, over the years we have had our share of heartaches: losing a loved one prematurely; seeing a child or an adult suffering and not being able to change things for them; sometimes being disappointed with someone in whom we thought we had seen the promise of great things. Yes, life bruises us at times, but often these kinds of experiences give us perspective and understanding and compassion.

Aging teaches us that true freedom comes not from hanging on, but from letting go. It is clinging to what is no longer life-giving that enslaves us. Of course, it should be clear that letting go is not the same thing as giving up. Sad indeed is the situation of someone who has given up on life and simply endures one day after another.

Aging gives perspective. It can become a time of self-realization, when we come to know ourselves in a way we never had before. For so much of our lives centrifugal forces draw us away from our true center. Old age can be a time of centering in which we find our deepest identity, our true selves.

Have you ever been a caregiver for a relative or friend who was dying and struggling with memories of the past? Were you careful to listen to that person and show your concern and your willingness to help in any way you could?

Reaching old age can become an important time of mending fences, of repairing relationships that may have become tattered over the years. It can be a time for reconciliation and forgiveness for the past failures—whatever they may have been and whomever they may involve. All this calls for courage: a willingness to talk about things that have for a long time been avoided, such as painful memories, hurt and buried feelings. Caregivers can be helpful at times in dealing with these hidden but not forgotten issues.

The later years of life can also be a time of joyful hope in a transcendent future, a future with God. They can be, for those who believe, a time to prepare, not morbidly but realistically, for that final transition to what Sidney Carton in *A Tale of Two Cities* called "a far, far better life than I have ever known before." For people of faith impending death takes on a positive meaning as we experience the presence of God and answer God's call to enter into the fullness of eternal joy.

Personal Data File

In addition, life's later years are the appropriate time to make sure that you have prepared (if you have not already done so) a "personal data file." This file will furnish the necessary information and the documents that will be needed by those who will care for you in case of your incapacitation or death. Make sure you include the following necessary information:

- A list of your bank account(s), credit cards, investments, insurance policies, any financial indebtedness.
- Basic facts about yourself: your birth certificate, your social security and Medicare numbers, your mother's maiden name, wedding and divorce documents, military service records, etc.
- A list of the people you wish to have notified of your death.
- Your desires for your funeral arrangements including the funeral director, the wake, the funeral service, the place of burial. Funeral arrangements should be part of your estate planning and can be made in advance. (One should consult a funeral director or a lawyer as to how this can be done.)

If your funeral service includes a Mass, you might want to indicate the music you would like, the readings, the presider, the homilist, readers and communion ministers. You might even want to designate the pallbearers you wish to carry your coffin. You probably would not want to go as far as the woman who requested only women pallbearers.

She explained: "Men don't seem to want to take me out now, why should I let them take me out then?"

If you wish to be cremated, you should write a statement indicating that this is your intent. If you wish to donate organs after you have died, you should fill out a donor card and make this information available to family members (see page 38). (For the church's teaching on cremation and organ donation, see part one of this book.)

Necessary Documents

• Documents such as your birth certificate, your will (drawn up with the help of your attorney), and your power of attorney designation.
• Your health care advance directives, which include: (a) living will, (b) health care proxy, (c) DNR directive (if this is your wish).

Once you have drawn up these documents, it is important to share and discuss your end-of-life wishes with your family, loved ones and your primary care provider. Besides communicating your own wishes, you may feel the need to take the initiative with a family member or a loved one who has not shared her end-of-life wishes with anyone. Since it may happen that a person in the prime of life can suddenly become incapacitated, it is never too early to begin talking about the way in which one would want to spend his or her final days. It is important that a person's wishes in this regard be put in writing—and shared with the appropriate persons. The National Hospice Foundation, in researching end-of-life care, found that Americans are more willing to talk about safe sex and drugs with their children than to discuss end-of-life care with their terminally ill parents. It is estimated that only 24 percent of Americans put in writing how they want to be cared for when they become terminally ill. The National Hospice and Palliative Care Organization (NHPCO) estimates that for every hospice patient, there are two more who could have benefited from the services offered by hospice, if they had known that such care was available.

Power of Attorney

A power of attorney is a document that empowers a person of your choosing (your agent or attorney, in fact) to act in your stead for purposes outlined in the document. This

Whatever your age, should you be giving thought now to preparing this type of file for yourself? Should you also take the time to share this file with the person or persons whom you wish to act on your behalf in case of your incapacitation or death? Such advance care planning is especially important for people who have chronic medical conditions, such as emphysema, diabetes, cancer, heart failure and the like. If such advance care planning has not been done, and these people become critically ill, physicians and other caregivers will not know their wishes and how best to deliver care suited to their desires.

document gives your agent the power to make decisions for you, if you become mentally incapable of making such decisions for yourself. The document may be a general power of attorney, which encompasses legal, financial or medical issues, or it may be a limited power of attorney encompassing only the issue or issues that you specify.

The Living Will

Advances in medical technology have made it possible to keep alive, by artificial means, persons who formerly would have died. Today life-support measures can keep a person's body alive indefinitely—even if brain function has ceased. At times treatments of this sort may be temporary measures that can lead to the restoration of health; at other times, however, these treatments may simply prolong the dying process without any appreciable benefit to the person.

Competent adults have the right to decide whether to begin or to continue or to terminate such treatments. A problem arises when you are no longer competent to communicate your wishes. That is why it is important that, while you are fully competent, you make out a "living will." The "living will" is a written document in which you express your wishes regarding the use of life support systems. The document details the conditions under which a person would no longer want aggressive treatment and would be satisfied with comfort care that would enable him or her to live out life's last days as free from pain as possible. The living will serves several purposes: It insures that your desires regarding withholding or withdrawing life-sustaining measures will be carried out. It is a guide for your loved ones and physicians that offers them assurance that they are doing what accords with your wishes. It preserves your own dignity and the carrying out of your choices when you are no longer able to express them. Remember, you can change this at any time and that it is valid only when you do not have the capacity to make your own decisions.

Health Care Proxy

In conjunction with the living will, it is important also that you designate a health care proxy whose responsibility it is to see that the provisions of your living will are carried out. The appointment of a health care proxy gives your agent the right to make decisions for you

The true measure of a society is how it cares for its dying.

—Mother Teresa

when you are no longer able to make them yourself. It is important, too, to authorize your proxy to have free and open access to all your medical records and all pertinent health-related information.

It is important that your proxy realizes that you are asking him to do what you want, not what he wants or what makes him comfortable. The proxy need not be a family member, but someone you believe understands your wishes and would honor them.

DNR (Do Not Resuscitate) Order

A do-not-resuscitate order directs the medical staff and those caring for you not to attempt to revive you if breathing or heartbeat has stopped. This means that physicians, nurses and other caregivers are not to initiate such emergency procedures as mouth-to-mouth resuscitation, external chest compression, electric shock, insertion of a tube to open the patient's airways, injection of medication into the heart, or open chest heart massage. If the patient is in a nursing home, the DNR order instructs the staff not to perform any of the above procedures and also not to transfer the patient to a hospital for such procedures.

The Last Stage of Aging: Terminal Illness[30]

I want to discuss the meaning of terminal illness by putting a question to you. How long do you want to live? Would you perhaps answer: "as long as possible"? As you know, the average lifespan now is somewhere in the seventies and is still being pushed back farther and farther, as science makes it possible for people to survive longer and longer.

How About Methuselah?

The Hebrew Scriptures speak of the early ancestors of Israel surviving for hundreds of years, with Methuselah topping them all with a record of 969 years. These num-

"Thus all the days of Methuselah were nine hundred and sixty-nine years; and he died."

—Genesis 5:27

bers are probably not meant to be taken literally, but for the moment let us reflect on them as if they were to be taken at face value. One wonders what quality of life Methuselah experienced at age 69 (for the average lifespan then was much shorter than today)—and, remember, whatever quality of life he may have had at 69, he still had 900 years to go! The very thought boggles the mind. Even today we know that after 69 (or thereabouts, depending on the person) it does happen that our physical abilities gradually begin to be impaired. Our system starts to shut down a bit—slowly perhaps, but relentlessly. For example, one day we meet a person we have known all our lives and, for the moment at least, we cannot, if our life depended on it, bring that person's name up from our memories. Such experiences should not be alarm us. They are part of the process of aging.

Sibyl of Cumae

There is an interesting Greek myth about the Sibyl of Cumae, a prophetess who is spoken of in Virgil's *Aeneid*. A clever lady to all appearances, her prophecies, we are told, were inscribed on palm leaves. According to legend, she offered nine volumes of prophecies to Tarquinius Superbus, the last king of Rome. He thought the price was too high. He refused to buy them, whereupon she burned three volumes and offered him the remainder at the same price. When he again refused, she burned three more. Finally, realizing that he had been outwitted, the king bought the remaining three at the original price.

I tell this story simply to suggest that the Sibyl of Cumae appeared to be a rather clever and wise prophetess. But there is another famous story about her that indicates that she was not as wise as she seemed to be. The story says that the god Apollo once offered her anything she wanted if she would take him as her lover. She accepted. Apollo asked her, "What do you want?" Her request was that she be able to live as many years as there were grains of sand in a pile of sweepings. These were counted and they numbered a thousand. So she was asking for survival that would go even beyond Methuselah's 969 years!

But sadly for her, what she never thought to ask for was the gift of continued youth. So what happened to her? A character in Petronius's racy novel *Satyricon* claims to have seen her with his own eyes: in her cave, tiny, all shriveled up and hanging from the ceiling of her cave in a bottle.

Children would come into the cave and, ironically, ask her the same question Apollo had put to her: "What do you want?" In a voice, weak but full of desperation, she would cry out: "I want to die! I want to die!"

Because she had the gift of many years, but not the gift of continued youth, she grew older and older, weaker and weaker. The diminishment that inevitably came with such fullness of years made death a desirable reality for her, but she had foreclosed that possibility for a thousand years. Though she had outwitted the king of Rome, she herself had been outwitted by the god Apollo. She had learned that mere survival is not necessarily a desirable choice.

When I asked you how long would you like to live, I was really asking: What kind of survival will suit you? Do you want to survive at all costs, as long as possible? Or would you feel that, at a certain point, life's quality would be so diminished that you would prefer to die?

Obviously I am not talking about the taking of one's life, and certainly not about assisted suicide. I am talking rather about the point in life about which you have decided you want no extraordinary measures taken to keep you alive. Enough is enough, you say. The time comes when mere survival is not a meaningful choice.

Caring for the Terminally Ill

Medical Care

Recent decades have witnessed a rapid growth of medical science and the development of sophisticated medications and procedures that can often cure many diseases that, until recently, had been fatal. In the case of the terminally ill, life can be prolonged much longer than had previously been possible.

This progress in medical science, wonderful as it is, creates problems of its own. All too often death comes to be seen, not just as a normal part of life, but as a challenge to be overcome or an enemy to be staved off as long as possible. Patients become cases to be solved rather than persons to be cared for. In such an atmosphere it becomes (at least this is what many believe) a medical necessity to utilize every possible treatment that might help to prolong the life of the patient.

But should one treat a medical capability as always a human necessity? This question, as well as other issues connected with so many spectacular scientific discoveries, has given birth to a new branch of ethics (or moral theology), namely, bioethics. Bioethics is the study of the ethical and moral implications of new biological discoveries and biomedical advances.

It is important to realize that Catholic moral teaching has never said that mere life is an absolute good, not even the highest good. Nor does it hold that death is the greatest evil and therefore something to be avoided at all costs. Saint Paul did not hesitate to write: "For to me, living is Christ and dying is gain" (Philippians 1:21). There are times when a greater good will justify the giving up of one's life. In such a situation, death is not chosen, but is allowed to happen for the sake of a greater good. The history of the church (especially in its earliest years) is filled with stories of women and men who chose to declare their faith even when it meant certain death.[31] The supreme example of choosing a higher good and allowing death to happen is Jesus on the cross laying down his life for the salvation of the world. This is the Jesus who said: "No one has greater love than this, to lay down one's life for one's friends" (John 15:13).

While it is not the highest good, still it should be obvious that life is a great good and must be respected. This means that every reasonable means to preserve life must be taken. It is not morally permissible for a person to take deliberate measures that would bring about his or her death. Suicide is morally wrong. Euthanasia is morally wrong. Yet the question must be asked: Is there a difference between taking one's life and choosing not to take all possible measures to prolong one's life? Is the latter equivalent to suicide or could it be seen as a situation in which a reasonable weighing of the circumstances in a particular case might rule out any obligation of taking extreme measures to prolong life? The question then becomes: How do you determine what measures would be considered normal (and obligatory) and which extreme (and not obligatory)?

Prolonging Life

Catholic tradition has never supported vitalism, the view that life must be preserved by all possible means, at any cost and no matter what the situation. From as early as the sixteenth century, Catholic theologians had accepted the distinction between ordinary and extraordinary means for prolonging life as satisfactory terms for designating what was obligatory and what was not. "Ordinary" means are those medications or procedures readily available, while "extraordinary" means are those that are expensive, difficult to obtain or involve a great burden for the patient.

This distinction once seemed clear and easily applicable. But the development of new and more complicated medications and medical procedures has made it more difficult to distinguish what is ordinary from what is extraordinary. For instance, before the development of anesthesia, a surgical procedure might have saved a life, but it would have involved intense pain and, therefore, would have been considered extraordinary. One could submit to such surgery, but was not obliged to do so. With the development of anesthetic surgery, procedures that offered reasonable hope of success became ordinary. Still, the overall situation of the patient must be considered in discerning what is ordinary or extraordinary. Giving intravenous fluids to someone who will probably recover is morally different from giving such treatment to a person who is dying.

Because human life is a great good, the presumption exists that it should be prolonged. But this presumption ceases if the means to prolong life are ineffective or if they involve a grave burden in a particular case. It is impossible to draw up a list of what is ordinary and what extraordinary that would apply in all cases. Each situation has to be judged on its own merits. Because of the difficulty of distinguishing ordinary from extraordinary, some have chosen to use different terms, comparing "benefits" and "burdens," or "proportionate" and "disproportionate" means of treatment. Richard A. McCormick has summed up this approach: "Briefly, if a proposed treatment will offer no benefit or if the benefit will be outweighed by the burdens, the treatment is morally optional."[32] Jesuit Reverend Thomas O'Donnell has pointed out that when artificial nutrition and hydration are withdrawn from a permanently comatose patient with an irreversible disease, the withdrawal of the medical treatment is not the cause of death. "The cause of death is the irreversible disease, which has caused both the coma and the inability to eat and drink....Thus, rather than causing death, their withdrawal accurately could be viewed as letting inchoative death occur."[33]

The International Congress in Rome

From March 17–20, 2004, the International Congress of the Pontifical Academy for Life and the International Federation of Catholic Medical Associations met in Rome to consider the issue of "Life-Sustaining Treatments and Vegetative State: Scientific Advances and Ethical Dilemmas."

A month before the meeting, Bishop Elio Sgreccia, the pope's top adviser on bioethics and vice president of the Pontifical Academy for Life, gave a talk in which he expressed the opinion that artificial hydration and nutrition for patients in a persistent vegetative state (PVS) is "simply care," and not medical intervention. His statement flies in the face of "the many statements to the contrary offered by medical societies, individual bishops and conferences of bishops," said Dominican theologian, Father Kevin O'Rourke.[34] As I have already pointed out, it has never been the position of Catholic teaching that physical life must be prolonged at all costs.

About a month after Bishop Sgreccia's talk, the International Congress met. On March 20, the last day of the meeting, Pope John Paul II spoke to the members of the congress. (In discussing the pope's address, it will be helpful to clarify some terms. What is the meaning of the term persistent vegetative state (PVS)? See below for some helpful definitions.

Coma—a state of "unarousable unresponsiveness" where there is no response to external stimuli. It may last as long as six months, but it will resolve itself either by an emergence into consciousness or a development into the persistent vegetative state.

Persistent vegetative state (PVS)—The persistent vegetative state is a form of deep unconsciousness. The cerebrum, the upper part of the brain, gives evidence of impaired or failed operation; it is this part of the brain, in its cortex or outer layer, which is responsible for those activities that we recognize as specifically human. The brain stem is still functioning in the PVS patient. It is this part of the brain that controls involuntary functions, such as breathing, blinking, involuntary contractions and cycles of waking and sleeping. PVS patients may open their eyes, respond to loud noises or go through cycles of waking and sleeping, but these activities are not indications of purposeful human activity. The brain functions at an involuntary level sufficient to continue life processes, such as respiration, digestion and sometimes swallowing. The PVS patient is not dead, nor should the patient be described as a "vegetable." The term "vegetative" is an indication of the level of functioning, not an indicator of the personhood of the individual. The person is human, but cannot perform distinctively human functions. He or she cannot interact with other persons.

Sometimes the letter *P* in PVS means "persistent"; other times it means "permanent." A vegetative state is considered *persistent* if it lasts more than a month. If it lasts more than a year, it is called *permanent*.

The pope began by pointing out that "the complex scientific, ethical, social, and pastoral implications [of the clinical condition called the vegetative state] require in-depth reflection and a fruitful interdisciplinary dialogue, as evidenced by the intense and carefully structured programme of your work sessions." As an important element of that dialogue, the pope went on to express his teaching on the issue:

> Our brothers and sisters who find themselves in the clinical condition of a "vegetative" state retain their human dignity in all its fullness.... The sick person in a vegetative state, awaiting recovery or a natural end, still has the right to basic health care (nutrition, hydration, cleanliness, warmth, etc.), and to the prevention of complications related to his confinement to bed.[35]

In his talk, the pope made the following points:

1. Being in a vegetative state does not diminish "the intrinsic value and personal dignity" of a person. "A man [sic], even if seriously ill or disabled in the exercise of his highest functions, is and always will be a man, and he will never become a 'vegetable' or an 'animal.'" Even those in a vegetative state "retain their human dignity in all its fullness."

2. "The administration of water and food, even when provided by *artificial* means, always represents a *natural* means of preserving life, not a medical act." To withhold it would be euthanasia by omission.

3. "Its use should be considered, in principle, ordinary and proportionate, and as such morally obligatory, insofar as and *until it is seen to have attained its proper finality,* which in the present case consists in providing nourishment to the patient and alleviation of his suffering" (emphasis added).

4. Positive actions need to be taken "against pressures to withdraw hydration and nutrition as a way to put an end to the lives of these patients."

5. It is necessary to give support and pastoral aid to families with a loved one in such a condition.

It is difficult to follow the pope's reasoning here, when he suggests that *artificial* means should be considered *natural* means. How can what is "artificial" be equated with what is "natural"? This position, however, has to be put in the context of Pope John Paul II's vigilant defense of life, both at its beginning and at its end, and his serious concern—a concern we should all share—that health care providers not fall into the fallacy of "euthanasia by omission."[36] The deepest issue, initiated by this congress and calling for further careful and prayerful discussion, is whether or not actions or omissions carried out in the case of a terminally ill person are efforts to prolong life, or, something very different, to prolong the act of dying.

Of great interest is the fact that a couple of weeks after this congress, on April 7, 2004, Bishop Elio Sgreccia felt it necessary to state that the pope's remarks had been wrongly interpreted by some to mean that a feeding tube is obligatory in every circumstance. When the pope spoke of "the proper finality" of nutrition and hydration, the bishop said, he was making an important qualification. They leave a "margin of judgment" to doctors and other health care professionals who must decide whether the feeding tube is achieving its "proper finality," namely, whether the patient is truly being nourished and having his suffering alleviated.

How is one to understand Bishop Sgreccia's statement? How are we to understand the terms he uses? It seems reasonable to suggest that "proper finality" may be read as an alternative for comparing *benefits* ("whether the patient is being truly nourished") and *burdens* ("whether the patient is having his sufferings alleviated"). This appears to be what Bishop Sgreccia means when he says:

> As long as nutrition and hydration are a support, as long as it is food and thirst-quenching drink that helps avoid suffering, it is obligatory. If the patient no longer assimilates food and if the patient no longer has thirst quenched by fluids but is only tormented, there is no longer an obligation to administer it.[37]

Karen Ann Quinlan

A case that may have been in the minds of some of the delegates to the congress was the much-publicized case of Karen Ann Quinlan. This twenty-one-year-old woman passed out at a party and stopped breathing. She was resuscitated and put on a respirator while still in a coma.

Eventually her condition was described as a permanent vegetative state (PVS). Her family accepted her prognosis as hopeless and sought advice from their parish priest. He assured them that the removal of the respirator was in full accord with Catholic tradition. The case generated so much publicity that Lawrence B. Casey, the bishop of Paterson, New Jersey, felt constrained to issue a public statement fully supporting the family in their decision to remove the respirator. Her physicians did not agree with the family decision and the case went to court. The New Jersey Supreme Court decided in favor of the Quinlans and named Karen's father as her guardian with the right to choose a physician who would carry out the wishes of the family. Ironically, Karen Ann Quinlan survived for ten years after removal of the respirator.

Terri Schiavo

A more recent case is that of Terri Schiavo, whose husband and parents fought about the issue of disconnecting her from the feeding tube that kept her alive for fifteen years. In February 1990, Terri Schiavo experienced a heart attack so severe that, in the best medical judgment, it placed her in a permanent vegetative state. Her husband, Michael, asked that the feeding tube be removed. Terri's parents, Robert and Mary Schindler, however, objected, holding out the possibility that she was capable of some recovery. Repeatedly, the courts sided with the husband. On October 15, 2003, in accordance with the courts' judgments, Terri's feeding tube was removed. Five days later, the Florida legislature passed a bill called Terri's Law, which permitted Governor Jeb Bush to intervene and have the feeding tube reinserted. This he did—to the conster-nation of constitutional scholars who saw this as an assault on the separation of powers.

The Catholic bishops of Florida issued a statement that appeared ultimately to favor the parents' position, as they called for further medical evidence before proceeding to a decision. They admitted that there are times when "one may refuse treatment that will result in a precarious and burdensome prolongation of life." They concluded by urg-ing more medical treatment "if it would be helpful to her condition."

On February 23, 2004, the Florida Supreme Court unanimously declared Terri's Law unconstitutional. In December of that year, Governor Jeb Bush asked the United States Supreme Court to review that decision. The Supreme Court declined. The case even brought an attempted intervention by a committee of the U.S. Congress, but the ruling of the Florida Supreme Court stood.

After some thirty-seven court reviews, state and national interventions, and after having her feeding tube removed and reinserted three times, Terri Schiavo died on March 31, 2005.

In June 2005 an autopsy performed by Dr. Jon R. Thogmartin revealed that Terri's brain had atrophied to half the normal size. The damage was irreversible. No amount of therapy or treatment, the medical examiners said, could have reversed her condition. Her eyes, in the famous videotape shown so widely and frequently in the media, saw nothing. She was blind. A sign once seen at a demonstration read: "How can you kill someone while she's smiling at you?" Now we know beyond any doubt that Terri Schiavo could not smile.

It seems clear that the continuous use of a feeding tube to keep Terri Schiavo alive must be seen as extraordinary means and therefore not obligatory in traditional Catholic moral theology. In the words of the *Catechism of the Catholic Church*, such means would be "disproportionate to the expected outcome" (2278).

Inevitably, the Schiavo case raises further questions: Was this primarily a moral issue or did it become an ideological and political one, in which the person of Terri Schiavo was almost lost? Yet a second question comes to mind as I recall the words of Saint Paul quoted earlier: "For me life is Christ, to die is gain." Were the efforts being made simply to keep Terri Schiavo alive physically actually delaying her entrance into the eternal life God has prepared for her and for all of us? As I have already pointed out, it is completely opposed to Catholic moral tradition to hold that physical life must be preserved at all costs. After all, we do believe that the life we are all ultimately destined for is immortal life with God. Or do we have to ask ourselves: Do we really believe this?

Palliative Care of the Terminally Ill

In the last decades of the twentieth century a revolutionary change has taken place in the care given to the terminally ill. There has been a movement from mere medical care to "comfort care or palliative care." This new approach to the care of the terminally ill was something I learned about some thirty-five years ago.

On June 5, 1968, I was in London, England. I remember the date well for it was the twenty-fifth anniversary of my ordination. Before going to Ely where I was staying with a friend, I had dinner at a small restaurant near Liverpool Street Station. I was happy to be alone, for being by myself gave me time to reflect on the experience I had had that afternoon. I had been to the Hackney district of London, where I visited St. Joseph's Hospice. Although the modern hospice movement grew out of the work of Dame Cicely Saunders, a British physician, who opened St. Christopher's Hospice in London in 1967, St. Joseph's Hospice has provided compassionate care to the dying for almost a hundred years. On July 2, 1900, at the persistent request of Father Peter Gallwey, five Sisters of Charity from Ireland came to Hackney. It was Father Gallwey's dream to provide care for people living in dire poverty in the tenements of Hackney and Hoxton. Contagious diseases and malnutrition were widespread. Grace Goldsmith, local benefactress, offered three hundred pounds a year to make that dream a possibility. On January 15, 1905, St. Joseph's Hospice opened to care for the poor and especially the terminally ill in East London. It continues to flourish today. It is run as a charity, welcoming people of every faith or philosophy, and is now supported by local health authorities (which cover about one-third of their costs) and fund-raising events, donations and legacies.

St. Joseph's Hospice, London

When I arrived at St. Joseph's, I was cordially greeted by one of the Sisters of Charity, Sister Paula, and given a tour of the building. As I walked through the wards where the patients were, I was deeply impressed. The wards were bright and lightsome. Lovely plants and fascinating fish aquaria gave a homey, welcoming touch. People were in bed or in chairs or wheelchairs. Some were reading, others knitting. There were no telephones ringing, no loud-speaker calling out doctors' names. No one appeared to be in pain. All was calm, bright and cheery. At the end of the tour I wanted to ask: "When am I going to see the people who are terminally ill?" But, of course, it was precisely the terminally ill whom I had just visited.

The sister invited me to join her for tea in one of their small dining areas. She told me of the mission of St. Joseph's. Its concern is, first of all, to respect the unique dignity of every person who comes there, whatever one's culture or religious beliefs are. The goal of the hospice is to enable all its patients to reach their full potential. This involves respecting their autonomy and encouraging them to participate in their own care. It also involves dealing with the patients' total pain, whether physical, mental, social or spiritual.

It means, too, encouraging open and honest communication with patients and their families, while at the same time respecting the patient's confidentiality and her or his wish to question or to remain silent.[38]

I asked the sister if St. Joseph's made any provision for people who wanted to die at home in familiar surroundings where they felt more at ease and more in command. She told me about St. Joseph's Community Palliative Care Team that was founded in 1975. The team includes doctors, clinical nurse specialists and social workers as well as volunteer helpers—all who minister to people in their home settings. There is also a team of experienced healthcare assistants available day or night to give families and caregivers some time of relief.

Hospice: A Growing Movement

The original meaning of hospice goes back to the Middle Ages, wherein hospices were places (generally monasteries) where travelers or pilgrims could stop for rest, food and shelter, or for help if they were sick or dying. There were hundreds of these hospices spread throughout Europe. They were often used by pilgrims on their way to the Holy Land.

Since 1967 the hospice movement as a way of caring for the terminally ill has had a remarkable growth. It has gone a long way in enabling people to see the dying process in a more enlightened and positive way. It has helped physicians and nurses (indeed all of us) to see that terminal illness should not be seen as a failure on the part of the medical profession; on the contrary, it offers the opportunity of moving, at the appropriate time, in a new direction and with different goals: from attempting to cure an illness to a commitment to care for the person who is ill. Palliative care can help to assure quality of life while dying—quality of life for both the person who is ill and his or her family. At the center of hospice philosophy of care is the belief that death is a natural part of life and the conviction that every person has a right to die pain-free and with dignity. It is also concerned to see to it that families will receive the necessary support that will allow this to happen. As Cicely Saunders and Mary Baines have written: "The aim is no longer cure but [instead giving the dying person] the chance of living to his [or her] fullest potential in physical ease and activity and with the assurance of personal relationships until he [or she] dies."[39] It would be wrong, therefore, to think that once curative measures are abandoned, nothing is being done for the dying person. Once curative medical treatment has been set aside as no longer appropriate, the attention moves to the kind of healing that the terminally ill have a right to. Cicely Saunders has put it so clearly:

> There are important ways in which we heal our patients and in which they heal us. Healing a person does not always mean curing a disease. Sometimes healing means learning to care for others, finding new wholeness as a family—being reconciled. Or it can mean easing the pain of dying or allowing someone to die when the time comes. There is a difference between prolonging life and prolonging the act of dying until the patient lives a travesty of life. At St. Christopher's, we offer people space in which to be themselves. We hold fast but with open hands; because sometimes the most important part of loving can be knowing how and when to let go.[40]

Two Awesome Moments: Birth and Death

What the hospice movement teaches us is the realization that what happens in the ending of a person's mortal life needs to receive the same loving and tender care as we give to a person at the beginning of life. Here is the way an anonymous poem has expressed it:

> When God sends forth a spotless soul
> To learn the ways of earth,
> A mother's love is waiting here;

We call this wonder birth.

When God calls home a tired soul,

And stills a fitful breath,

Love divine is waiting there,

This, too, is birth, not death.

As the poem makes clear, there is a sacredness about life in its beginning. We approach the coming into this world of a new person with a deep sense of awe and humility. The same reverence and respect need to mark our attitude toward the dying process that ushers a person out of this mortal life into life eternal. "The pains of dying may be seen as labor pains for the mysterious release of the spirit, much as labor in pregnancy prepares for the miracle of birth."[41] A concrete example of a small, privately run home for the dying is the Isaiah House in Rochester, New York. Kathy Quinlan, nurse and director of Isaiah House, describes that precious moment that ushers a person from mortal life to life eternal: "The dying time is like no other in its remarkable potential to expand and deepen life's meaning and blessing. And yes—it is a gift time!"[42]

Cicely Saunders and St. Christopher's Hospice, London

Small homes for the dying like Isaiah House have sprung up in many places.[43] There are also the larger institutional hospices, such as St. Joseph's and St. Christopher's in London, England, and many others throughout the world. Many hospitals now offer hospice care to those for whom it is appropriate. I have already spoken about St. Joseph's Hospice. No writing on hospice would be complete without an account of Cicely Saunders and all she has done to promote this movement that has done so much to bring comfort and peace to dying persons and their families. As Sandol Stoddard has written:

> The beginning of the modern hospice movement in England was placed on a very firm foundation: a national health service; a long, commonly recognized, and state-approved religious tradition; and the innovative brilliance of British pharmacology. Above all, there was the towering genius of Dame Cicely Saunders, and the loyalty of her many gifted colleagues, such as Dr. Thomas West....Dr. West wrote recently (1987): "Twenty-one years ago a one-woman, interdisciplinary team opened St. Christopher's and began the worldwide hospice movement. Dame Cicely brought her nursing, social work and medical skills with her and, it should be added, her Christian convictions." This affectionate tribute rings with truth and at the same time suggests a problematic challenge to those in other countries who in very different settings have since set out to do hospice work.[44]

One of Saunders's important contributions to heath care was her introduction into the healing vocabulary of the term "total pain." Total pain is a holistic approach to understanding terminal illness (or indeed any illness) that looks not only to the physical elements of suffering, but also to its psychological, social, emotional and spiritual aspects. These latter may at times be more burdensome than the physical suffering itself. Such an approach calls for understanding something of the uniqueness of each person. It involves narrative, biography and hearing the patient's story as a way of opening up problems and issues that otherwise would never come to the surface.

What Is Palliative Care?

Palliative care means alleviating the symptoms of a disease without curing it. The word "palliative" has an interesting derivation. The Latin word *pallium*[45] means a "cloak that covers something over." So palliative care cloaks cover the disease a person is suffering; that is to say, it covers over the disease by dealing, not with the illness itself, but with the symptoms caused by that illness. When symptoms are adequately controlled, a good quality of life can be achieved for the person who is ill and for his or her family.

Palliative care, it should be noted, is not restricted solely to people who are dying or enrolled in hospice care. As the Institute of Medicine wrote in 1998: "Palliative care seeks to prevent, relieve, reduce or soothe the symptoms of disease or disorder without effecting a cure." It can apply to people who have an illness that is incurable, but not necessarily one that is immediately life-threatening. The judgment about the employment of palliative care rests with the individual, physician(s), primary caregiver and the hospice team, where the expected outcome of such a judgment is relief from distressing symptoms, the easing of pain and the enhancing of the quality of life.

Dorothy H. Summers, who works at St. Christopher's Hospice in London, gave a talk in 1979 at a Science Morality Conference at Nazareth College, Rochester, New York. She spoke about the importance of dealing with the symptoms of illness and quotes one of the patients at St. Christopher's: "Here you do not chase away the pain, you anticipate it."

Over the years since the founding of St. Christopher's, great strides have been made—not only in England, but also in the United States and elsewhere—in the development of sophisticated ways of dealing with symptoms. Kathy Quinlan has described the treatment used at Isaiah House and elsewhere: "Most patients are now treated with a skillful combination of a long-acting medication plus immediate-release analgesia for in-between (breakthrough pain) that may be given every one to two hours as needed."[46] Dr. Ira Byock maintains that pain can *always* be alleviated.

> What my profession dryly calls "symptom management" involves not only a pharmacopeia of medications (palliative care has advanced far beyond the old morphine-based Brompton cocktail), but also a collection of aggressive symptom-relieving techniques. Within the hospice pharmacopeia, a large array of medications (from glucocorticoids to anticonvulsants, antidepressants, and even psychostimulants) are remarkably useful when applied to specific pain syndromes. Modern medical technology and advanced pharmaceuticals have given doctors the ability to reliably ease the physical discomfort of terminal illness.[47]

In her talk at the Science Morality Conference, Dorothy Summers pointed out that once physical pain has been adequately diagnosed and properly cared for, there is a need to look at other issues that influence the patient's experience of pain.

A fearful, anxious patient may often complain of excessive physical pain but does not find it easy to express his anxieties. We have to learn to be good listeners; sitting close to patients and in silence that only the patient should be allowed to break can be a threatening experience for us, but it is invaluable to patients who are trying to find the courage to express their fears. Accepting death as being part of life, allowing dying patients to remain in the ward and not pushing the bed into a side room, and letting others see death as peaceful and that we shall be with them can be very helpful.[48]

She points out also the importance of helping the patient work out the social and spiritual pain that will generally accompany the dying process. The patient, as well as the family, experiences bereavement: the parting with loved ones. Perhaps the greatest stress faced by patient and family is the "conspiracy of silence" that so often surrounds death and prevents people from facing the inevitable future and sharing their feelings about it together. Even allowing the dying person to share with the family decisions for the family's future can help to bring peace and tranquility to all. There is also the spiritual pain. Without ever forcing one's own convictions on the patient, caregivers and families must listen with support and concern to the patient's anxieties about the future both of the patient and of the family left behind. The caregiver is not an answer-giver, but a sincere and sympathetic listener. Again to quote Dorothy Summers, "One of the greatest securities a hospice can offer is that the patient and family will never be turned away and that staff will journey with them to the end of the patient's life and on into bereavement for the family."[49] The family will continue to be helped in their time of bereavement after the patient dies.

The Revolutionary Nature of the Hospice Movement

Hospices and homes for the dying have revolutionized the approach of caregivers to patients. One doctor is reported to have said: "This is wonderful. At last I have the time to get to know the people I am working with, and time to spend with the patients. It's what I have been waiting for all my life." Another doctor said: "It's a life-changing experience for a physician to become involved in hospice. My patients now see that I understand their pain, that I have something to offer them. I stay with them and we talk. In the past, I never gave out my personal telephone number to patients and their families; now I always do. I want them to know that they can call me and that I really care for them. And I feel loved in turn, now by my patients."[50] This doctor goes on to say that involvement in hospice has affected all his relationships, including those in his own marriage and in his family. His whole life, he says, has taken on new meaning. Hospice is ongoing "intensive care." Cicely Saunders on one occasion was giving a group of visitors a tour of St. Christopher's. One of the visitors asked her: "Where are the intensive care units?" Her reply summed up the meaning of hospice. She said: "Why all our units are intensive care!"

Hospital and Hospice Compared

Perhaps one way of understanding the revolution that hospice has brought about is to compare hospice with hospital.

Both have the same etymological source. For both are derived from the Latin *hospes*, which means "guest" or *hospitium* which means "a guest house." One way of describing the contrast between the two is to suggest that "hospital" is masculine and "hospice" is feminine. By that I mean that the hospital tends to bring out in both men and women their masculine side: the hospital is oriented toward solving cases, dealing with problems, making well those who are sick. Hospice, on the other hand, calls forth the feminine qualities in nurses and doctors and other caregivers: namely, the qualities of nurturing and caring. Hospitals, it could be said, are concerned with the illness a person has; hospice with the person who has the illness. Hospitals are committed to curing, hospices to caring. This is not to deny that hospital personnel are caring people. It is simply to point out a very different emphasis that helps define the two.

While the hospice movement had its beginnings in England, it came into existence in the United States in the mid-1970s and quickly spread throughout the country. In fact, it was Cicely Saunders's visit to Yale University in 1967 that helped inspire interest in the hospice philosophy that would soon begin to thrive in many places in the United States. Most hospice care is given in the home, though institutions, such as hospitals, may also give hospice care.

If Cicely Saunders may be regarded as the leading figure in the development of the hospice movement in England, it can be said that Elisabeth Kübler-Ross played a somewhat similar role in the United States. Born in Zurich, Switzerland, she graduated from medical school at the University of Zurich in 1957. The next year she came to the

United States. In the New York hospital where she worked, she was appalled by the standard treatment of dying patients. "They were shunned and abused, nobody was honest with them," she said. Unlike her colleagues, she made it a point to sit with terminal patients as they opened their hearts and told their stories to her. She began giving lectures, telling the stories of terminal patients and what they had gone through.

Her book *On Death and Dying* established her as an internationally renowned author. She said that she wanted to break through the layer of professional denial that prohibited patients from airing their deepest inner concerns. She encouraged people to look at the dying process in a positive way and to see the hospice movement as embodying such an outlook. In her book she sought to see a pattern of stages by which the dying come to an awareness of their terminal illness.[51] These stages are five: (1) denial and isolation, which occurs when the patient (or her loved ones) first learns that she is terminally ill. A kind of numbness sets in as well as a sense of disorientation, hysteria: "This cannot be happening to me (or to him or her)"; (2) anger, which may be directed at God ("Why is God allowing this to happen to me?") or may show itself in envy of others who are enjoying life, while the patient experiences pain and the realization: "I am dying, but others are not"; (3) bargaining, with God or with life: "If I am good, maybe the terminal nature of my illness will be postponed," or "perhaps I can live to see my daughter get married or my son graduate from college"; (4) depression, which involves a realization of what one must give up and let go of and the feelings of loss and sadness that accompany this realization; and (5) acceptance, becoming aware that death is inevitable and a desire to get the most out of the time that remains.

How Hospice Care Works

In the United States hospice care is most often given in the home; typically a family member will serve as primary caregiver. Members of the hospice team will make regular visits to evaluate the patient's condition and provide whatever care services are called for. The hospice team—which includes physicians, nurses, social workers, clergy or other counselors, trained volunteers, even speech, physical and occupational therapists, if needed—is an interdisciplinary team. It develops a plan for each patient: a plan that will manage pain and symptoms control. It provides whatever drugs, medical supplies and equipment may be needed. One of its important tasks is to instruct the family on how to care for the patient. Respite time for the family must be worked into the schedule of patient care. Trained volunteers also form a part of the hospice team. When the patient dies, bereavement care and counseling are provided for the surviving family members.

Here is a description of Isaiah House (mentioned earlier) that may be seen as typical of the small, privately run home for the dying:

> Staffed primarily by volunteers—even our physicians are volunteers—Isaiah House continues to offer hospitality and comfort care to two dying persons at a time. Preference is given to those whose economic and psychosocial resources are lacking or who are unable to

remain in their own homes. Over and over again, our cadre of compassionate caregivers quietly, unassumingly, and ever so tenderly minister to, wait with, and say goodbye to our residents. And in those countless vigil times, something quite wonderful is possible. If we can be open to the grace of these moments, we can learn to face, even to embrace, our own mortality and recognize that death is a normal part of our lives and a most unifying human experience.[52]

Family Involvement

Family and friends also play an important role in bringing comfort to the dying. Dr. Ira Byock has written: "To be certain that the people we love do not become statistics of the crisis in end-of-life care, we family members and friends must retain responsibility to care for those we love as they die."[53] He points out also, very concretely, the responsibilities that belong to society and to local communities to see that the needs of dying persons are met.

Of the fundamental needs of persons as they die, only the need to control physical symptoms is uniquely medical. Their more basic needs are broader than the scope of medicine. They need shelter from the elements, a place to be. They need help with personal hygiene and assistance with elimination. They need nourishment or, as death comes closer, sips of fluid to moisten the mouth and throat. They need companionship, and they need others to recognize their continued existence.

In recognizing these needs we can say to the dying person with our words and, more importantly, with our actions: "We will keep you warm and we will keep you dry.

We will keep you clean. We will help you with elimination, with your bowels and with your bladder function. We will always offer you food and fluid. We will be with you. We will bear witness to your pains and your sorrows, your disappointments and your triumphs; we will listen to the stories of your life and will remember the story of your passing."[54]

Medicare Hospice Benefit

In 1983 important legislation passed by the United States Congress, called the Medicare Hospice Benefit, made it possible for the terminally ill over sixty-five to qualify for Medicare. Obviously this increased the ability of hospices to respond to the needs of the terminally ill. To date more than 90 percent of hospices in the United States are certified by Medicare. To be eligible for Medicare Hospice Benefit, one must fulfill the following requirements:

- The patient must be eligible for Medicare Part A.
- The patient's physician and the medical director of the hospice must certify that the patient is terminally ill with life expectancy of six months or less.
- The patient must sign a statement indicating that he or she has chosen hospice care instead of standard medical benefits for the terminally ill.
- The patient must select a Medicare-approved hospice care place or program.

The Medicare Hospice Benefit covers the following hospice services: skilled nursing care, physician's visits, skilled therapy, home health aid visits, medical social services and nutritional and spiritual counseling as well as bereavement support for the family. It also provides drugs for pain management and respite care to relieve the care-giving responsibilities of the family. The Medicare Hospice Benefit is a most generous program: There are virtually no out-of-pocket expenses for drugs, equipment and other high-cost items often needed for the terminally ill. The National Hospice and Palliative Care Organization on its Web site explains more specifically what Medicare provides.

• Medicare pays the hospice program a *per diem* rate that is intended to cover virtually all expenses related to addressing the patient's terminal illness.
• Because patients require differing intensities of care during the course of their diseases, the Medicare Hospice Benefit affords patients four levels of care to meet their needs: Routine Home Care, Continuous Home Care, Inpatient Respite Care and General Inpatient Care.
• Ninety-six percent of hospice care is provided at the routine home care level, which is reimbursed at approximately $114 per day.
• The Hospice Benefit rates have increased annually based on the Hospital Market Basket Index. With the advent of costly new drugs and treatments like palliative radiation, the average cost to hospices has risen much faster than the hospice reimbursements rates.
• Hospices that are Medicare-certified must offer all services required to palliate the terminal illness, even if the patient is not covered by Medicare and does not have the ability to pay.

The National Hospice and Palliative Care Organization (NHPCO)

In 1978 the National Hospice Organization (which in 2000 changed its name to the National Hospice and Palliative Care Organization) entered the picture as a strong advocate for the terminally ill and their families. Its headquarters are at 1700 Diagonal Road, Suite 625, Alexandria, Virginia 22314 (phone 703-847-1500). It develops educational materials and programs to spread knowledge about the meaning and availability of hospice and palliative care. It convenes meetings and symposia on issues related to such care. It also conducts research, monitors congressional and regulatory activities and works closely with other organizations interested in end-of-life issues.

Making Hospice Care Better Known

Today there are forty million seniors in the United States. Over the course of the next thirty years that number will double as baby boomers reach the age of sixty-five. This is a generation that has emphasized living well. They will be equally concerned to die well. Palliative care and hospice as a provider of palliative care provide the quality of life that allows people to live well as the end of life draws near. While information about palliative care and hospice is spreading, there is still is a high percentage of people who do not know about it. I have read that the percentage is as high as 83 percent of the American people. In 1999 hospice care was provided for at least 700,000 people, up from 540,000 the previous year. This is a small number when statistics show that about 2.4 million Americans die each year.

It is a sad fact that 40 percent of people referred to hospice care die within seven days of admission. Earlier referrals would ensure that patients and families will have access to the benefits that hospice is able to give.

The Pastoral Care of the Terminally Ill

The experience of dying brings people face to face with their own mortality. It can be a daunting experience that may move them to look at their spiritual capital and wonder how ready they are for the inevitability of death. The church wants to be present to help them deal courageously with their situation and to bring them a sense of peace and serenity in the realization that they face death not alone but as part of the Christian community. The sacrament of the anointing of the sick is one of the seven sacraments of the church. It is a sacrament that in the past was often misunderstood, for it was thought of as part of a series of rites called the Last Sacraments that were reserved for those who were actually dying. Relatives or friends hesitated to call the priest, lest the patient feel that they were facing the immediacy of dying. The Second Vatican Council changed all this. It reordered our thinking

> *From the General Introduction to the Rite:*
>
> *"Great care and concern should be taken to see that those of the faithful whose health is seriously (perilously) impaired by sickness or old age receive this sacrament."*
>
> *A prudent or reasonably sure judgment, without scruple, is sufficient for deciding on the seriousness of an illness (8).*

about this sacrament in two important ways. First, it clearly restored an earlier (pre-medieval) understanding of the sacrament that saw it as a ritual whose purpose was to strengthen those whose health was debilitated by illness or old age. Thus, it is not a signal to the dying person that he or she is about to die; rather it is a gift of God's healing grace seeing people through a difficult time in their lives.

From the General Introduction to the Rite:

The sacrament may be repeated if the sick person recovers after being anointed and then again falls ill or if during the same illness the person's condition becomes more serious (9).

The second thing the Council did was to restore the communal nature of this sacrament. It involves the participation of the whole Christian community and the ministry of the sick to that community. In this context Pope Paul VI's apostolic letter, promulgating the new rite, made clear that this sacrament of anointing is not only a ministry *to* the sick and the dying; it is also a ministry *of* the sick and the dying. Their ministry is to bear witness in the church to the frailties of human life and to the deeper realities of human existence: those realities that all too often are lost upon so many people involved as they often are in a whirlwind of activity that gives them little time to reflect on the realities that are of ultimate importance. The sick and the dying are witnesses to the compassion of Christ so evident in the wonderful healing miracles he performed during his public ministry. They are a sign of Christ's healing ministry in the midst of the Christian community.

The scriptural evidence for this sacrament is found in the Letter of James:

Are any among you sick? They should call for the elders *[presbyters]* of the church and have them pray over them, anointing them with oil in the name of the Lord. The prayer of faith will save the sick, and the Lord will raise them up; and anyone who has committed sins will be forgiven. (James 5:14–15)

It should be noticed that this passage does not speak about those who are "on the point of death," but simply those who are sick. This means that any one of the faithful, when their lives are endangered by serious sickness or old age, may be seen as appropriate candidates

From the General Introduction to the Rite:

A sick person may be anointed before surgery whenever a serious illness is the reason for the surgery (10).

for this sacrament. The liturgy begins with a Penitential Rite, followed by a Liturgy of the Word. The priest prays over and lays hands on the sick person and anoints him or her with the Oil of the Sick, which had previously been blessed by the bishop on Holy Thursday morning. If this oil is not available, the priest may bless oil before anointing the person. In the actual anointing ceremony, the priest anoints the person's forehead with the prayer: "Through this holy anointing may the Lord in his love and mercy help you with the grace of the Holy Spirit." The response is: "Amen." Then the priest anoints the hands, saying: "May the Lord who frees you from sin save you and raise you up." Again the response: "Amen."

As a liturgical rite, the anointing of the sick may take place at a Mass celebrated in the church or in the home or the hospital room of the sick person. In fact, in many places it has become a custom to celebrate with some regularity the anointing of the sick within a Sunday or weekday Mass.

If the anointing takes place at a Mass, after the ceremony of the anointing (described above), the priest continues with the Liturgy of the Eucharist. When Eucharistic Prayer II is used, after the words "and all the clergy," there is added: "Remember also those who ask for healing in the name of your Son, that they may never cease to praise you for the wonders of your power." In Eucharistic Prayer III, after the words "the family you have gathered here," there is added: "Hear especially the prayers of those who ask for healing in the name of your Son, that they may never cease to praise you for the wonders of your power."

From the General Introduction to the Rite:

Elderly people may be anointed if they have become notably weakened even though no serious illness is present (11).

Some Reflections on Who Can Be Anointed
- It is difficult to establish objective criteria as to who should receive the anointing.
- The emphasis should be placed on healing, rather than simply on the danger of death.
- It is not a sacrament for well people. So indiscriminate anointing of a whole congregation should be avoided.
- Age by itself is not an illness, though it is often accompanied by illness.

Perhaps the simplest way of putting this is to say that persons who are experiencing serious physical or mental suffering and feeling the need of healing can be considered as appropriate candidates for this sacrament.

What about chronic disease? Probably this condition is not normally a reason for anointing. But there may be times when someone with a chronic illness is struggling with the illness and experiencing the need for healing of body and spirit. In such situations they certainly could be anointed.

When in doubt, anoint. *Favores ampliandae sunt.*

Viaticum: The Last Sacrament

The last sacrament of the Christian life is not the anointing, but Viaticum: the reception of Communion by a dying person intended to provide him or her with spiritual food for the journey through death to eternal life (*via tecum,* "on the way with you," that is, "food for the journey"). This may be celebrated within a Mass or outside it. If outside of Mass, the minister may be a deacon or an unordained minister who regularly serves as a minister to the sick.

Catechesis

Besides the sacraments available to the dying, pastoral care would also suggest that there are times in the celebration of the liturgy, and especially in the service of the Word, when the Mass texts and the readings become appropriate occasions for speaking about the Christian meaning of death: that it is not an end but a way of entrance to new life. The material in part one of this book could be helpful in presenting this positive meaning of death.

Bereavement

Bereavement is the experience of loss. It could be the loss of some thing that is precious in your eyes, like a family heirloom or that indispensable appointment book. It may be the loss of a job (I write this at a time when many companies are "downsizing" and people who have enjoyed a job for years find themselves suddenly deprived of that job). It may be a relationship, once important to us, that has been lost because of irreconcilable differences. But bereavement takes on its strongest meaning when it applies to the loss through death of persons dear to us, such as a parent, a spouse, a child, a sister, a brother, a close friend, etc. Death robs us of our dear one (that is the literal meaning of bereave "to rob" or "take away"). The depth of the relationship or the circumstances in which the death occurs affects the way one grieves. There is a difference, say, between the sudden death of a child and the more or less anticipated death of an aged parent who for years has suffered dementia. Both are losses, but the grief they will call forth will be significantly different.

While we tend to think of bereavement as the experience of one who loses a person he loves, grief also applies to the loved one who is terminally ill and moving through the dying process toward inevitable death. Here too there is experience of loss and of letting go. The dying person has to let go of what was his normal pattern of life and of many social contacts that once had special meaning in his life. There is a narrowing of the ability to function in ways and situations that once had been quite normal: driving a car or traveling by plane cease to be possibilities. There is the learning to live with chronic pain. In a recent *Pickles* comic strip, the grandson asks his grandfather if he experiences pain when he gets up in the morning. He replies: "If I woke up in the morning without pain, I would probably be dead." Finally there is the final letting go—the letting go of mortal life in the experience of death.

Grief

There is a difference between grief and mourning. Grief refers to the inner feelings and emotions evoked by the loss of a loved one. Mourning is grief's external expression. "Grief refers to the feelings of sorrow, anger, guilt and confusion that can arise when you have suffered a loss or are bereaved."[55] Grief fluctuates from one emotion to another as one tries to deal with a seeming emptiness in her life caused by a loss that is irretrievable. Recovery is slow and emotionally draining. Each person must *work* through grief in her own way (and it is *work* that can drain a person's energy and emotional strength). The depth and character of the emotions will depend on the relationship one has had with the deceased as well as the age of that person. There may be feelings of denial: a refusal to believe that a loved one is really gone. Some have suggested that Elisabeth Kübler-Ross's different stages of the dying process (or at least some of them) may be helpful in understanding the grieving process. Thus, a person who has lost a loved one may react by simply refusing to believe that the loved one is really gone. Once reality sets in ("It's a fact that she has died. I cannot deny it."), the grieving person may grapple with the question: "Why did this have to happen to someone so dear to me?" Other feelings can surface: sadness and inability to get beyond constant preoccupation with thoughts about the deceased. A person may feel fatigue or loss of appetite. Taking care of life's ordinary, everyday tasks becomes difficult. But eventually the realization dawns that life must go on—and the loss must be accepted. All we have is the present. One cannot live—for very long at least—in a past that has ceased to be. Life will never be exactly the way it was before your loved one died. A deep faith can be helpful in the process of recovery from grief. A person who believes in God and in a divine goodness that goes beyond the grave can take comfort in the certain hope that a loved one has truly gone home to God and enjoys a happiness that nothing in this world could even approximate. Speaking to a spiritual mentor may be helpful, especially if the grieving person has confidence in that person and feels free to share his feelings. Speaking also to others who have experienced similar loss and sharing with them—becoming aware of others who have traveled through the same tunnel of darkness and come out at the other side—enables one to overcome a sense of aloneness in suffering. It is important, too, that those who are grieving should be patient with themselves, yet at the same time careful to avoid indulging themselves in feelings of self-pity. Healing takes time. It is a process that cannot be hurried. Moreover, it is not a time to make major life decisions. These should wait until a clearer sense emerges of what direction the future should take. If the grieving continues after the first-year anniversary of the death, a person may need to seek help. A good place to begin is to consult the family doctor or a spiritual guide. Getting help is especially important if one has continued difficulty in sleeping, experiences significant weight loss or gain or finds little improvement in the ability to function in the ordinary activities of daily life.

Mourning

Mourning may be thought of as all the actions and rituals we use to give external expression to our grief. Different cultures have different ways of mourning. Wakes and funeral services offer grieving persons acceptable cultural ways of acknowledging the loss they have experienced. These and other similar types of rituals also give friends and relatives of the deceased and of the grieving party the opportunity to offer comfort and loving concern for the bereaved. Among Catholics the ritual of the Mass, participated in by relatives and friends, is an unrivaled time for articulating the grieving person's feelings in the context of a familiar ritual that can lift us above the realities of this mortal life as we return a loved one to God. For some, visiting gravesides on special occasions and leaving flowers there can help keep alive a memory of our loved ones. Gradually, as time and God's grace touch us, our memories are less tinged with grief and sadness, as faith in the life to come gives us at last a sense of proper perspective on death and clearer understanding of the meaning of life.

Are there certain mourning rituals and practices that are a part of your family tradition and important to you? Has the dying person communicated her or his wishes in this regard to you or to the appropriate person or persons involved?

Sudden and Unexpected Death

In another *Pickles* comic strip the grandson asks his grandmother what she is reading. She tells him, "*People* magazine." "Why is it then," he asks, "that you have the Bible on your lap?" She answers, "Just in case." He asks, "Just in case what?" The grandfather chimes in, "She doesn't want to be found dead reading *People* magazine. So she keeps the Bible within grasping range." One way, though probably a not very convincing one, of guarding against an unprovided death!

There are times when death comes suddenly and unexpectedly. A person may die in an automobile accident or a fire or from a fatal heart attack or from another unforeseen calamity. While sudden and unexpected death may relieve a person of the suffering that normally precedes death, it deprives that person of the opportunity of taking care of issues he perhaps would have wished to deal with. It also plunges loved ones left behind into a premature and completely unexpected experience of grief. That is why, in the Christian tradition, the litany of the saints always includes a petition: "From sudden and unprovided death, deliver us, O Lord." There is also a prayer for a happy death:

> O God, great and omnipotent judge of the living and the dead, we are to appear before you after this short life to render an account of our works. Give us the grace to prepare for our last hour by a devout and holy life, and protect us against a sudden and unprovided death....Teach us to "watch and pray" (Lk 21:36), that when your summons comes for our departure from this

> world, we may go forth to meet you, experience a mer-
> ciful judgment, and rejoice in everlasting happiness. We
> ask this through Christ our Lord. Amen.[56]

Being plunged into sudden and unanticipated grief is especially difficult to handle. In such situations, all that is said above about grieving would still apply, though, without any time to prepare, initial emotional reactions to sudden death may be more intensive and may especially require thoughtful family members and friends to offer emotional, psychological and spiritual help to assuage the suddenness and intensity of the experience.

Anticipatory Grief

Normally, grief follows loss and involves the effort to learn to live without that which has been lost, whether that means a person or a thing or an object dear to the one who grieves. But it can also happen that grief precedes loss in anticipation of it. This is what is referred to as anticipatory grief. Anticipatory grief is not a substitute for the grief that follows the death of a loved one, nor does it necessarily lessen the post-death experience. What it does do is to help prepare one for the emotional, psychological and spiritual experiences that come when the actual loss occurs.

Anticipatory grief is not a single experience; rather it involves a number of losses. Thus, it may be concerned with the *past* (shared events that can never be experienced again); the *present* (seeing the diminution of a loved one's capabilities, for instance, her inability to communicate adequately and clearly), the *future* (foreseeing the loneliness and the emptiness of life that will eventually come with the death of the loved one).

The intensity of anticipatory grief will depend on a number of factors: the relationship and degree of intimacy between the griever and the one who is dying; the griever's age, maturity and ability to cope with difficult situations; and, by no means least, the faith the grieving person has in a God whose love will give eternal life to the one who is dying and whose healing power will comfort those who mourn.

The danger in anticipatory grief that needs to be dealt with is the possibility that it may lead to a premature detachment from the dying person that may produce a kind of emotional numbness. Then, when death does occur, grievers find it difficult to express the true depth of their feelings. Others may misunderstand and misinterpret this as apathy or insensitivity.

Care for Caregivers

Caregivers want to offer the best possible care for their loved ones who are dying. It is important that they not try to do too much alone. They need the help and cooperation of professional and volunteer health care personnel. Caregivers can expect to experience a wide range of stressful emotions. Failing to deal with these emotions can easily lead to burnout, where there are feelings of guilt that they are not doing enough for their loved ones or feelings of helplessness in the face of the inevitable. *It is important that the caregivers not forget to take care of themselves.* They will take better care of their loved ones if they take better care of themselves. This means that they need time for rest. They need to take breaks for themselves to rejuvenate their own spirit. Volunteers who serve on the health care team can be most helpful in giving them "time off." In the long run the caregiver who takes time off for herself (and not just for necessary chores) will be better equipped physically, psychologically and emotionally to give her best efforts to the care of the dying person whom she loves.

When Children Grieve

In *The Seven Storey Mountain,* Thomas Merton narrates how, when he was six years of age, he received a letter his mother had written from her hospital bed, telling him he would never see her again. Much later, as a Cistercian monk, he recalled: "I took the note under the maple tree in the back yard and worked over it, until I made it all out and had gathered what it really meant. And a tremendous weight of sadness and depression settled on me."[57] It was a time when children were given little information about terminal illness and were not allowed to visit patients in hospitals. It was also the time when it was beginning to become the usual practice for most patients to die in hospitals instead of at home.

It is a natural desire on the part of adults to protect children from anything that might cause them pain. Should they be told about death? Those who know the story of Siddhartha Guatama (who would become the Buddha) will remember how his father tried to protect him from anything that would cause him pain or discomfort. His father's plans ultimately failed because—as was inevitable—he finally saw sickness and death and this is what led him to embark on his search for the solution to the problem of suffering. Since death is an inescapable reality in human life, sooner or later children must be told.

It is better that they be told before death comes close to them in one whom they love.

It may be that they are able to handle death better than many adults are. Young children see members of their families come and go. As their siblings grow up, children see them in different contexts. They see brothers and sisters leave to go to college or to get married. They understand that their relationship with family members is frequently changing. Approaching life with little preconceptions, they can generally deal rather easily with such different types of relationships. They are able to bring this somewhat casual approach even to death. William Wordsworth has captured this perception of a child in his simple poem "We Are Seven." The poet tells how he

> met a little cottage Girl:
> She was eight years old, she said;
> Her hair was thick with many a curl
> That clustered round her head.

The poet asks her how many sisters and brothers she has. She answers:

> Seven are we;
> And two of us at Conway dwell,
> And two are gone to sea.
> Two of us in the church-yard lie,
> My sister and my brother.

The poet tells her: Then, if two have died, there are only five of you. But she persists. No, there are seven. For, she tells him, she often goes to the churchyard, where the graves of her sister and brother are fresh with green and

there she knits and sews. Sometimes she takes her por-
ringer and eats her supper there and sings a song to them.
The poet still insists that they are only five, for two are
dead. But the little girl will have none of it,

> The little Maid would have her will,
> And said: "Nay we, we are seven!"

This young child, at least in the poet's view, had an intu-
itive understanding of the continuity of human existence
that not even the grave can break.

Most young children probably do not experience
death in a significantly personal way. Obviously there are
exceptions. Perhaps their first meaningful exposure to
death may happen with the death of a grandparent, which
can happen any time in their childhood. Younger children
find it difficult to see death as irreversible: People die, but
some day they will come back. By the time they get to
school, they begin to realize, without always understanding
perfectly, that death is irreversible, that it is universal, and
that it is personal. Parents need to be honest with their
children and give them correct knowledge of what death
means. This must be done in ways appropriate to the children's age and in language they are able to process.
Theresa M. Huntley, in her excellent book *Helping Children
Grieve,* has written:

> One of the earliest childhood fears is separation from
> caregivers. Young children are not able to differentiate
> between a short, temporary absence and a long, possi-
> bly permanent one. Any separation can cause them
> anxiety. We can alleviate some of this fear by building

> positive separation experiences into children's lives.
> Begin with very short periods and then gradually
> lengthen the time you are away. Leave the children with
> someone they know and trust.... After you return
> home, spend some time with your child to see how your
> time away from her went.[58]

The religious and cultural context that exists in the family
will enter into the way death will be perceived by children.
If a family believes in life after death (that is, with the
understanding of death presented in part one of this
book), it may well be a comfort to the child to know that
grandma and grandpa will be united with one another in
heaven with God. Barbara Johnson narrates the story of a
young boy who was dying from cancer. He asked his
mother: "What is it like to die? Does it hurt?" His mother
reminded him of what it was like when he fell asleep on the
way home from a visit to his grandparents. "When you
woke in the morning, you found that you were in your own
bed, because daddy had carried you into the house and to
your bed." "Death is like that," she told him. "You fall
asleep here and you wake up and find that your Father has
carried you home."[59]

Jan Seeley, a Montessori teacher in Syracuse, New York,
told me of one very concrete way of helping children deal
with death. Here is her story.

> My Montessori preschool suffered the loss of our pet
> hamster. I didn't know how I was going to break the
> news to the children who loved the cuddly creature and
> were entertained by its antics. I prayed that I would rec-
> ognize the "right moment." Ten minutes after dismissal,

a sudden, unexpected and uncharacteristic quiet came over my classroom of twenty-five three- to six-year-olds.

"Boys and girls I have news for you," I began. I deliberately did not want to prejudge that it would be sad news, bad news, good news, etc. "Do you remember that living things need air in order to breathe? Well, Chubby stopped breathing. He couldn't get air anymore."

Three children immediately got the message and threw themselves into my lap, weeping. One by one, other children who felt sad spontaneously lined up for their turn to be consoled. Some just stayed in place, watching the others and pondering what this news actually meant. We began to recall funny stories about Chubby, such as the time he escaped from his cage and was finally captured on the third day.

We laughed and cried.

After recess a few children immediately went to the art area and chose to make drawings for Chubby, which they hung on the wall. They asked if they could get a new pet. "Not right away," I said. "We can't always replace something, or someone, that dies."

Someday we will get a new pet, but I wanted to teach them a lesson about death: not to try to replace it with something living, but to feel the loss and grieve over it and then let others console them.

How fortunate these little ones were to have a teacher so sensitive to their needs, who was able to take an experience they had together to prepare them for the day when they would be grieving at the death of some person whom they loved.

Dealing with all the issues involved in the grief that children experience is a topic that all by itself needs study and reflection. Parents need to take advantage of ordinary situations in life in which dying is seen as a part of life, for instance, the flowers dying in the garden, the changing of the seasons, the death of the family dog or cat. If children are made to realize that it is all right to talk about death, they may feel freer to ask the questions that come to them. It is unwise to tell children only half of the story, such as saying that grandma has gone away or is asleep. Nor should they be told that God loved grandma so much that God took her to be with God. This can raise doubts about what is meant by God's love. Religious teachings about the meaning of life and death, however, can be helpful to the child. One can teach them that life has a higher meaning, that we are called to carry on the work of a loved one who has died, that we can do good works in memory of that person.

Should children be taken to wakes and funerals? This is not an easy question to answer and may differ with the age and character of the children. Normally, though, it seems better that children be with their families during a time of grieving, rather than kept away from them.

There are a number of books on the subject that parents and other caregivers will find helpful in speaking about death with children. In addition to Huntley's *Helping Children Grieve*, some books will be included in the bibliography.

❧ PART THREE ❧

THERE

WHAT ETERNAL LIFE WILL MEAN FOR US

May He support us all the day long,
till the shades lengthen,
and the evening comes, and the busy world is hushed,
and the fever of life is over, and our work is done!
Then in His mercy may He give us a safe lodging
 and a holy rest, and peace at the last.[60]
—*John Henry Newman*

Death, as we have seen, is our final act of total freedom, in which—in the light of God's grace—we choose what our eternal destiny will be. Catholic teaching offers us three possibilities: hell, purgatory, heaven. I want to begin with the most undesirable of the three. Then I propose to give the greatest attention to the most desirable.

What Do We Believe About Hell?

What about persons who don't make it to heaven or purgatory? Is there a hell of everlasting punishment? Some would suggest: It's better to believe in it, just in case it might be true. Remember Blaise Pascal (1623–1662) and his "immortal wager"? Even if there is only one chance that God exists—and that hell is a possibility—and ten thousand chances that God does not exist...choose God, and thus insure yourself against the hazard of damnation.

For many centuries Christians lived with a sin-centered religion and belief in a severe punishment-prone God. These people firmly believed in hell, and most of them figured they would probably end up there. This seems to have been especially true in the Middle Ages, perhaps also in the seventeenth century. Barbara Johnson's book tells of a man who had just had surgery and, as he came out of the anesthesia, he asked the surgeon "Why are the blinds drawn, Doctor?" The doctor answered, "There was a big fire across the street, and we didn't want you to wake up and think the operation was a failure."[61]

The gnawing, morbid fear of hell as a real possibility in one's life lingered well into the twentieth century. For instance, in the 1940s and 1950s (to choose just one specific period), when people went to a parish mission or a school retreat, they waited with apprehension, yet also with a kind of morbid curiosity, for the "hell and brimstone" sermon—standard fare for such events that they knew would come sooner or later. A classical example of this genre of sermons is the retreat talk of Father Arnall in James Joyce's *A Portrait of the Artist as a Young Man*. Stephen Dedalus, after an evening's visit to a brothel, returns to school, and the next day must go to the annual retreat. Father Arnall in his homily on hell describes at great length and in lurid detail the reality of hell and the suffering experienced there.

Several years ago I gave a retreat at Maggie Valley in North Carolina. I remember on my way back home listening to a tape of *A Portrait*. It was a creepy experience driving seventy miles an hour through the mountains of North Carolina and listening to this depiction of hell. Here are brief excerpts:

> Now let us try for a moment to realize, as far as we can, the nature of that abode of the damned, which the justice of an offended God has called into existence for the eternal punishment of sinners. Hell is a strait and dark and foul smelling prison, an abode of demons and lost souls, filled with fire and smoke.... The prisoners are heaped together in their awful prison, the walls of which are said to be four thousand miles thick and the damned are so utterly bound and helpless...that they are not even able to remove from the eye a worm that gnaws at it....
>
> All the filth of the world, all the offal and scum of the world shall run there as a vast reeking sewer.... The brimstone, too, which burns there in such prodigious quantity fills all hell with its intolerable stench....
>
> But this stench is not, horrible that it is, the greatest physical torment to which the damned are subjected. Place your finger for a moment in the flame of a candle and you will feel the pain of fire.... The sulphurous brimstone which burns in hell is a substance which is especially designed to burn forever and forever with unspeakable fury.... Every sense of the flesh is tortured and every faculty of the soul therewith; the eyes with

impenetrable utter darkness, the nose with noisome
odors, the ears with yells and howls and execrations, the
taste with foul matter, leprous corruption, nameless, suf-
focating filth, the touch with redhot goads and spikes,
with cruel tongues of flame.[62]

Listening to these morbid (I want to say obscene) words of
Father Arnall, as I sped through the lovely North Carolina
countryside, was something of a trip back to yesteryear.
And what I quoted above is just an excerpt from that grue-
some sermon that goes on much longer. Stephen leaves
the chapel, convinced that he is condemned to hell. In
that frightening sermon, he heard nothing of a forgiving
God eager to reconcile sinners, only of a God who punishes and punishes ruthlessly.

Hell and a Different Understanding of God

Today in a religious context that tends to emphasize love
as the essential element of Christian living and love as the
basic meaning of God, the very notion of a hell of everlasting punishment is something that many Christians find
not so much threatening as profoundly disturbing, even
problematic.

In the context of the Gospel and the universal saving
love of God, hell must be seen as a self-chosen state of
alienation from God rather than as punishment inflicted
by God. God does not reject the sinner, but the sinner can
reject God. Hell supposes a complete turning away from
God. It must be viewed as the opposite of heaven: heaven
as eternal communion in love with God and all the saints;
hell as utter aloneness in a self-chosen isolation. Heaven

means being drawn finally and completely out of oneself in love. Hell is to be utterly absorbed and trapped in oneself. T.S. Eliot puts into verse this sense of aloneness.

What Is Hell?

Hell is oneself,

Hell is alone, the other figures in it

Mere projections. There is nothing to escape from

And nothing to escape to. One is always alone.[63]

A variation on the same theme is in Jean-Paul Sartre's play, *No Exit.*

So that's what Hell is: I'd never have believed it…

Do you remember brimstone, the stake, the grid-iron?…What a joke! No need of a gridiron, Hell is other people.[64]

Yet we must never think of hell as an equal alternative to heaven. Scripture texts that speak of heaven and hell are not to be interpreted in an overly literalistic way. The descriptions of judgment, heaven and hell are not eyewitness accounts. Hell is described in the Scriptures as a real possibility of being finally lost and estranged from God— by the free choice of rejecting God's love. Hell must never be thought of as vindictiveness on God's part, but as the radical choice of the creature to reject the creator.

In German legend Dr. Faustus is an alchemist who sells his soul to the devil in return for occult powers. Only in death does he realize the disastrous choice he has made. Christopher Marlowe (1564–1593) reflects on that choice in his play *Dr. Faustus:*

> Why, this is hell, nor am I out of it:
> Thinkest thou that I who saw the face of God
> And tasted the eternal joys of heaven,
> Am not tormented with ten thousand hells
> In being deprived of everlasting bliss?

Some theologians have questioned whether or not the possibility of losing everlasting bliss can ever become a reality. Many see the conception of hell as what John Shea calls "the cultural picture of another time."[65] Today he says the possibility of hell seems to equal the possibility of annihilation. For hell is total isolation from all that is. It is rejecting God and that means rejecting being itself. Rejecting being itself is to choose nonbeing or nothingness.

Hell as Annihilation

To put this another way: at death, a person's false self disappears, the true self cannot be affirmed, as there has been no effort all through life to affirm it. This means that the true self that a person might have been no longer exists. Death for such a person means nothingness. It makes sense then to see death in such a situation as simply annihilation, simply ceasing to be.

Karl Rahner has pointed out that the true significance of the doctrine of hell is to be found in what it tells us about human existence here and now in this life. Marie Murphy sums up Rahner's teaching about human existence:

> In Rahner's understanding, hell must be understood as the drive toward self-autonomy. Human beings are endowed with freedom. Rahner defines human free-

dom as the power to decide that which is to be final and definitive in one's life. It is through our freedom that we either accept or rebel against that which is the essence of our creaturehood, that is, self-surrender to the incomprehensible mystery that is God. Every moment of our lives is a stage on the way to this final goal of self surrender.[66]

This understanding of hell—as a drive toward self-autonomy and independence of God—is a reality that exists here and now in this life, on both an individual and even a cosmic dimension. To quote Marie Murphy again:

This understanding of hell is much more menacing. Hell is now and hell can be forever. We have the power to set ourselves in contradiction, in all the dimensions of our being, from the community of humankind, from the cosmos and from God. We may choose to live the alienation and antagonism which is hell right now.[67]

Universalism

The church has never stated that persons actually go to hell or that there are persons now in hell. Today, in fact, there is even a drift toward *universalism*—a belief that has ancient Christian roots in Origen and in Gregory of Nyssa—namely, belief in the ultimate salvation of all peoples. This position is based on Christian hope in the power of God's grace—the belief that even human sinfulness is ultimately no match for God's saving grace: the saving grace of a God who wills all peoples to be saved. William J. Dalton writes, "The God of the [New Testament] is not half-saving, half-punishing. He is the God of salvation. God is a saving God, and if He can save all, then He will save all. We may have a real hope that all may be finally saved."[68]

The question needs to be asked, however: Does this make a mockery out of free will? Does it trivialize free will? Does it suggest that free will ultimately does not matter? These are deep questions that must be raised, even though we cannot give definitive answers to them.

What Do We Believe About Purgatory?

Many faithful Christians who try to live up to the gospel realize the imperfections that mar their lives. They don't anticipate immediate entrance into heaven. But with hope in God's mercy they have a reasonable expectation that, with a little bit of luck, they will end up in purgatory and hopefully for only a short while. What is purgatory anyway? It is a belief that is widely misunderstood, probably because it has been presented so inaccurately. The problem about much of our past teaching about purgatory is that *we have tended to contrast it with hell,* which is seen as a place of eternal punishment, whereas purgatory, by contrast, is a place of temporal punishment. The obvious difficulty with such an approach is that it casts God in a role that doesn't at all suit the God revealed to us by Jesus Christ. It is an approach that seems to say: When God forgives sin, God remits the eternal punishment due to sin (hence one is freed from hell). But God still exacts punishment because of the infraction of the divine will. This (temporal) punishment is suffered either in this life or in purgatory.

Just take a moment to reflect on this way of understanding purgatory. Surely it casts God in a very bad light: as One who is not content with our sorrow, but wants to exact punishment even after we have received forgiveness. This is hardly the God Jesus told us about. Just try to fit this notion of purgatory into the parable of the loving father and the prodigal son!

Purgatory as Purification

There is, however, another and much more meaningful way of conceiving purgatory. Instead of contrasting it with hell, we can *look at it in relation to heaven*. When we sin (and who of us does not?), sin leaves its vestiges. It leaves weakness and imperfection. When we come to the moment of death with these weaknesses and imperfections, we are not fully the persons God wills us to be. We are not yet fully our true selves. We need to be purified. Purgatory is the experience of that purification.

Those who have been brought up linking purgatory with temporal punishment may be surprised to learn that this concept seems to have yielded place to a more understandable way of thinking about purgatory. Purification makes more sense than punishment. It is worth noting that the *Catechism of the Catholic Church*, in its three articles on purgatory (1030–1032), speaks of purification and makes no mention of temporal punishment.

Some theologians would hold that this purification is instantaneous. It happens in the very moment of death. It is part of the experience of death. The intense ray of God's love penetrates our whole being and burns out of us the egotism that prevented us from giving ourselves wholeheartedly to God. Purgatory, as Hans Küng has expressed it so beautifully, is the "wrath of God's hidden grace."[69] For George Herbert, seventeenth-century English poet, this hidden grace is that Love divine that welcomes us to Love's table, regardless of how unworthy and unready we may feel.

> Love bade me welcome, yet my soul drew back,
> Guiltie of dust and sinne.
> But quick-ey'd Love, observing me grow slack
> From my first entrance in
> Drew nearer to me, sweetly questioning
> If I lack'd anything.
> "A guest," I answer'd "worthy to be here";
> Love said, "You shall be he."
> "I, the unkinde, the ungratefull? ah my deare,
> I cannot look on thee."
> Love took my hand and smiling did reply,
> "Who made the eyes but I?"
> "Truth, Lord, but I have marr'd them; let my shame
> Go where it doth deserve."
> "And know you not," says Love, "who bore the blame?"
> My deare, then I will serve."
> "You must sit down," says Love, "and taste my meat."
> So I did sit and eat.[70]

To move to a more prosaic source (already referred to above), I would point out that the *Catechism of the Catholic Church* in its initial draft, which was called the *Catechism of the Universal Church,* spoke of purgatory as "painful purification." Most interesting is the fact that the definitive version dropped the adjective "painful." Thus, the *Catechism* says: "All who die in God's grace and friendship, but still imperfectly purified, are assured of their eternal salvation; but after death they undergo purification so as to achieve the holiness necessary to enter the joy of heaven"

(1030). It goes on to say: "The Church gives the name 'Purgatory' to this *final* purification of the elect..." (1031).[71]

Note the *Catechism* says that they undergo this purification *after death*. This is, of course, to use a term that belongs to time to designate something that is outside of time. Death has a "before," but not really an "after." We use the phrase "after death" because we are conditioned to think in terms of "time" and "after" is a term of time. Death, however, terminates the temporal phase of our personal existence. Quite literally we can say that purgatory takes no time at all. For death puts us outside of time. Death is moving from a personal existence that is "in time" to a transformed personal existence that is "outside of time." That is why it seems eminently reasonable to me to speak of purgatory as simultaneous with death.

One way of thinking of the relationship of time to eternity is to see time as a circle and eternal life as the center of the circle. Each point on the circle relates to the totality at the center. This is one way of reflecting on the prayers we say for those who have entered through death into the very life of God. No matter what the point in time we may be in when we offer prayers for our loved ones who have gone to God, every point relates equally to the center. Thus the prayers I may say today or tomorrow or a week from now, all relate to the same eternity. To cite a simple example, the prayer I might say a week after a friend dies reaches into a timeless eternity and therefore may well be a source of strength for the friend in that decisive moment of death. This speaks to us of the engrossing mystery of time somehow impinging on eternity.

John J. Savant, in an impressively poignant article in *Commonweal,* writes of the death of his beloved wife. It was a devastating experience, one that burst the bounds of well-meaning clichés that friends often resort to in the hope of offering some bit of comfort. He yearns to discover some "compelling assurance of an abiding mutual need."

> And I do mean a mutual need. It is hard to imagine how a soul can be ready to pass from the last temporal flutter of breath to the deathless vigor of divine love. So much dross remains: the unresolved anger; the fear-spotted faith; the abiding vanity and stubborn prejudices. So much baggage impedes our entry into the kingdom prepared for us. That is why, as a dear nun recently reminded me, "The dead need us."
>
> I have found in this insight a guide to recovery and purpose. It tells me that my enduring vocation, as widower, is to continue to work on my marriage. This means that I must continue to console my beloved over our bodily separation—and seek consolation from her.[72]

It's as if John Savant has sought and perhaps found a way for time to touch on the mystery of eternity's timelessness.

Earlier I cited some metaphors for grasping the moment of self-discernment that takes place at death. Yet another metaphor is to see death into God as getting to know our true name for the first time: the name that alone expresses who we are. In the Book of Revelation the risen Jesus promises to those who listen to the Holy Spirit that "I will give a white stone, and on the white stone is written a new name that no one knows except the one who receives it" (Revelation 2:17).

Purgatory, therefore, may be seen as that experience of eternity, in which I come to know God and my own identity. It is the experience of hearing my own true name for the first time. It is receiving from the risen Jesus that white stone spoken of in the book of Revelation.

Rowan Williams, archbishop of Canterbury, tells the story of a famous rabbi who lived in Prague.[73] One night the rabbi had a dream in which he stood before the throne of God. Eagerly he asked the angel before the throne if his name was written in the book of the saved. The angel said: "I will read the names of all the people who died today and whose names are in the book of life." The rabbi listened, but his name was not called. He wept, for he could not understand why his name had not been read. The angel said to him: "I did read your name." "But I did not hear it," he insisted. The angel replied: "Many come here who through all their years on earth never hear their true name. They thought all along that they knew their true name but they did not. They have to stay here at the gate to the kingdom until they are able to hear their own true name."

Purgatory brings to an end that time of waiting, as at last God calls us by name and we hear that call for the first time and it tells us who we are.

Reincarnation

Reincarnation (the belief that after death a person's soul is reborn in another body) is especially linked with Eastern religions (Hinduism and Buddhism, for example), though through the centuries it has continued to crop up in the history of the West. According to Hinduism, continual rebirth takes place until the person's soul *(atman)* has been sufficiently purified and thus enabled to enter into nirvana, a state of bliss and perfection. What determines the type of body a person will be reincarnated in is his or her actions or *karma.* The notion behind belief in reincarnation is that normally one lifetime is not sufficient to overcome the effects of bad *karma.* In each new incarnation the person is purified and eventually "gets it right" and becomes worthy of eternal union with God *(Brahman).*

That a person needs to be purified of the weakness and imperfections of his or her life does offer Catholic thinkers a point of contact with the oriental understanding of purification. As has been stated above, purgatory is all about the purification that one must undergo to be readied for entrance into God's presence. But, as has also been pointed out, this purification takes place in the experience of death, not in a series of deaths, and returns to one or more additional earthly existences.

Reincarnation is a topic that seems periodically to make an appearance in a Christian context. The notion of the preexistence of souls is found in the writings of Plato, whose thought had considerable influence on early Christian teaching. One of the great theologians of the third century, Origen of Alexandria, steeped in Platonic thought, taught a doctrine of reincarnation that eventually was condemned by the Fifth Ecumenical Council—the Second Council of Constantinople in 553. Gnostic sects at various times have expressed a belief in reincarnation and at the present time it has proved to be quite fashionable in "New Age" religion.

Pope John Paul II, in his 1994 apostolic letter "As the

Third Millennium Draws Near" *(Tertio Adveniente)* suggests why this teaching has been so popular:

> How are we to imagine a life beyond death? Some have considered various forms of *reincarnation:* depending on one's previous life, one would receive a new life in either a higher or lower form, until full purification is attained. This belief, deeply rooted in some Eastern religions, itself indicates that man rebels against the finality of death. He is convinced that his nature is essentially spiritual and immortal.[74]

Some have sought proof of reincarnation in various texts of Scripture. To give but one example, consider the story in John 9, when Jesus cures a man who had been blind from birth. The disciples ask: "Rabbi, who has sinned, this man or his parents, that he was born blind?" The disciples consider the possibility that this man may have been guilty of the sin that caused his blindness. This could not have happened during his present life because he had been born blind. Thus, so the argument goes, the disciples' question presupposes a prenatal existence.

But it is easy to exchange Scripture texts. Thus, one could cite against reincarnation this text from Hebrews: "It is appointed for mortals to die *once,* and after that the judgment" (9:27, emphasis added). Pope John Paul II, in the letter cited above, makes clear: "Christian revelation excludes reincarnation, and speaks of a fulfillment which man is called to achieve in the course of a single earthly existence." Christian faith opposes any notion of reincarnation, because (1) it seems to deny the Christian belief that we are saved by the sufferings and death of Jesus

Christ; (2) it conflicts with the doctrine of the resurrection of the body; (3) it is based on a dualism that separates body and soul (a concept which, as we have seen earlier—in part one—is a Platonic notion but not a biblical one).

The belief in reincarnation is rejected in the *Catechism of the Catholic Church*:

> Death is the end of man's earthly pilgrimage, of the time of grace and mercy which God offers him so as to work out his earthly life in keeping with the divine plan, and to decide his ultimate destiny. When "the single course of our earthly life" is completed, / [*LG* 48§3] we shall not return to other earthly lives: "It is appointed for men to die once" [*Heb* 9:27]. There is no "reincarnation" after death.[75]

Limbo

A generation or more ago one of the most heartrending experiences of Catholic parents was their concern for the fate of a child who died without being baptized. The grief and sorrow of losing a child—an experience devastating enough in itself—was accentuated by the belief that an unbaptized child had no possibility of getting to heaven. In fact, if we want to go back much further than a few generations (some sixteen hundred years or so in fact), we find Saint Augustine teaching that those who die without baptism are condemned to hell. (In fairness to Augustine, he was defending the necessity of baptism against the teachings of Pelagius who asserted that baptism was not necessary for salvation, though this hardly gets Augustine off the hook for what can only seem [at least to us today] as a heartless position.)

Medieval theologians, in an effort to mitigate the harshness of that position, came up with the notion of limbo. Limbo, they asserted, was understood not as a place of punishment, but a place or state of natural happiness enjoyed by unbaptized children. They could never, however, attain to the supernatural happiness of the beatific vision.

Modern theologians tend to question the theological premises on which the notion of limbo rested. How is it possible to reconcile limbo with a loving God and God's universal salvific will? Quite simply put, the belief about limbo has no place in contemporary theological thought. Nor is it given any serious consideration in the church's official teaching. Thus the *Catechism of the Catholic Church* says:

> As regards *children who have died without Baptism*, the Church can only entrust them to the mercy of God, as she does in her funeral rites for them. Indeed, the great mercy of God who desires that all men should be saved, and Jesus' tenderness toward children which caused him to say: "Let the children come to me, do not hinder them" [*Mk* 10:14; cf. *1 Tim* 2:4] allow us to hope that there is a way of salvation for children who have died without Baptism.[76]

What Do We Believe About Heaven?

Recently in talking on the telephone with a friend, I mentioned that at the moment I was writing about heaven. His comment was: "One must not write about heaven except in a beautiful way. Such writing calls for poetry rather than prose." I found this comment very helpful and disconcertingly challenging. Heaven is beauty discovered and enjoyed forever. I shall try, though I am not at all certain that I am equal to the task of describing it in the language of beauty and poetry and sheer joy. Yet this is a task that

"All my life I've had no

doubt that life goes on

and have always been

so curious about

'what comes next.'"

needs doing because so many people who are sincere believers do not really think of heaven as beautiful or as particularly enjoyable. They are not at all sure that heaven, as they have heard it described, is what they want for their eternal future. They are somewhat like the little boy who, when asked to tell what heaven meant to him, said quite confidently: "Oh, I know what heaven is, but I don't want to go there. I want to go to North Carolina instead." I don't know any others who would want to choose North Carolina over heaven, but I suspect that in many cases the only reason people have for wanting to choose heaven as their final destiny is their uneasy feeling that they do not have any other option or that the only other option open to them is exceedingly unattractive. Heaven seems to be the only available way of avoiding hell.

How does one go about describing such indescribable beauty? Perhaps it is necessary to begin by admitting the inadequacy of human language to do justice to the topic. It is important to make clear that all the language we use to describe heaven is metaphorical or symbolic (though surely the metaphors or symbols should be, as my friend suggested, beautiful ones). Where do we get them? We draw them from the realities and experiences of this life that we find most appealing: realities and experiences that bring us happiness and enduring joy. What are these realities and experiences? Clearly, as history shows, they will vary from one era of history to another. What appropriately describes heaven for one age may not be satisfying to people of another age. Each age will draw on the realities and experiences which best describe what the happiness and enduring joy of heaven mean for them. But, as we reflect more on heaven and the imagery we use to clarify it, we realize in the end that heaven will always far exceed any and all the realities and experiences that our age or any other age in history has or will draw on to try to say what heaven really is. Try as we may, heaven's beauty is simply beyond all telling. There is nothing in our human experience that can adequately mirror the wonders of heaven. Heaven, when achieved, will always be a surprise! As I try to write this chapter, I think of a dear friend from Lincoln, Nebraska, with whom I used to correspond quite regularly. She discovered that she had cancer. At the hospital the surgeon removed a tumor from her stomach the size of a cantaloupe. Surprisingly the surrounding tissue was completely normal. The doctors recommended chemotherapy as a precaution. She wrote: "With the clean lab report I chose to go with a healthy body and immune system and a strong faith and a good mind rather than a program of pumping poisons into a body that has been so good to me." When her Presbyterian pastor tried to persuade her to follow the medical advice, she said to him: "You mean you don't really believe all that stuff we've been talking about? I'm going to bet my life on it." She confided to me: "All my life I've had no doubt that life goes on and have always been so curious about 'what's next.' Once when I was thought to be dying of pneumonia, I was excited that I was soon going to know and was disappointed later to wake up out of a coma." Our correspondence continued for almost two more decades. Finally cancer took her and now she knows what she had longed to know and what you and I can never know until we join her. I suppose if she were writing to me now she might well say: "So you're trying to write about heaven, are you? Forget it! You just don't have the vocabulary to do it. No matter what wonderful experiences you have had in your life, it simply can't compare with the happiness and joy that are mine now and forever. Have you forgotten Paul's words, in a text he borrowed from Isaiah, where he says that 'no eye has seen, nor ear heard, nor the human heart conceived, what God has prepared for those who love him' (1 Corinthians 2:9)?"

Yes, it seems clear that heaven is too much for mere human words to bear. Reading Dante is proof enough of that. Laura Gascoigne, in doing a review in the (London) *Tablet* (8:26:03) of an exhibit of paintings on Paradise in the National Gallery, put it well: "Readers of Dante's *Divine Comedy* will appreciate the difficulty of describing paradise in words. His *Inferno*? Gripping. His *Purgatorio*? Not bad. His *Paradiso*? Let's be honest: dull, dull, dull.[77] In a similar vein, it can be said that John Milton's *Paradise Lost* is far more engaging than his *Paradise Regained*.

Perhaps, then, I should stop right now and say I am not equal to the task of describing what comes after death and neither is anybody else. But, despite the impossible difficulties, I take courage to go ahead by listening to chapter sixty-eight of *The Rule of Saint Benedict*. In this chapter Benedict discusses a situation in which the abbot asks a monk to do some task, and it is clear to that monk that it is something that he simply cannot do. How should the monk deal with this issue? The Rule says he should represent to the abbot the impossibility of his being able to do what he has been asked to do. *Before reading further, take a few moments to reflect on what heaven means for you.* But, if the abbot insists, then the Rule simply says, "Do it anyway." So, I shall follow the spirit of that rule and proceed to examine some of the metaphors or symbols people have used at various times to describe heaven. But, please, be lenient with me and do not expect too much. Some of the symbols may appeal to you, others may not. In fact, if one of them strikes you as completely adequate, you may have made the serious mistake of turning the symbol into the reality. Each of the symbols says something about heaven. No one of them separately nor all of them together is equal to the task of describing the fullness of what heaven means.

An overly literalist interpretation of images of heaven leads to confusion. It is based on a misconception that wants to see heaven as a place outside our history and geography to which we go: like a choice vacation spot to which people go and are allowed entry if they have the proper reservations. This spatializing of heaven—as some place distinct from God and people, where God already is and where you and I hope to go someday—is a false image that distorts the whole meaning of the afterlife, the life of heaven. For heaven is not some place to go to. It is not a place where God is at home and to which hopefully we shall one day go to take up permanent residence as one of God's tenants. Heaven is simply God and God's people becoming fully one. Pope John Paul II, at his general audience of July 21, 1999, said that heaven, "is neither an abstraction nor a physical place amid the clouds, but a living, personal relationship with the Holy Trinity."[78] When this world has passed away, those who accepted God in their lives, and were sincerely open to His love, at least at the moment of death, will enjoy the fullness of communion with God, which is the goal of human existence."

Karl Rahner connects the meaning of heaven with the resurrection of Jesus. He makes the interesting point that when the Risen Jesus entered into glory with God, he was not entering into a preexisting place called heaven. Rather the Resurrection "established heaven" in its most radical sense. For Resurrection established the human possibility of union with God.

Heaven is the marvelous possibility within us of communion with God. In a sense heaven is not something we wait for. It is right here now: our communion with God is a reality already in process of being realized. As we move toward that total awareness of God that is our final destiny, heaven is already beginning.

Heaven as Homecoming

If you are Irish or of Irish descent, you probably know that the Irish have their own answer to the question "What is heaven?":

> A little bit of heaven fell from out the sky one day;
> And nestled on the ocean in a spot so far away

And the angels found it, sure it looked so sweet and fair;
They said, "Suppose we leave it, for it looks so peaceful
there."
So they sprinkled it with stardust, just to make the sham-
rocks grow;
'Tis the only place you'll find them, no matter where
you go
Then they dotted it with silver to make its lakes so grand;
And when they had it finished, sure they called it
Ireland

I have an Irish background. In 1954 I was there for a couple of weeks. I had never been to Ireland before, and I
have to go back two generations to locate someone of my
family who lived in Ireland and came to America. Still,
wherever I visited, the people I met asked me at the very
beginning of a conversation: "Ah, Father, when did you
come home?" The fact that my roots in the Emerald Isle
were somewhat remote didn't really matter. What counted
was that I had an Irish name. So I was immediately being
welcomed home. No matter how strange it may have
seemed to me at first, people made clear to me that *I had
come home.*

Home is the best metaphor for heaven.

Barbara Johnson's *He's Gonna Toot and I'm Gonna Scoot:
Waiting for Gabriel's Horn* has a lot of slapstick, off-the-wall
humor as well some good doses of wisdom. In her book
Johnson has a drawing that takes the shape of a note to the
reader. The note says:

MEMO:
Gone to the Father's home to
prepare a place for you.
Will be back soon to pick you up.
Jesus

The memo, of course, is the author's paraphrase of John's Gospel wherein Jesus says: "In my Father's house there are many dwelling places.... And if I go and prepare a place for you, I will come again and will take you to myself..." (14:2–3).

Homecoming is a useful symbol to prod our thinking about heaven. It is one that we can readily identify with. Homecoming is a frequent experience in our lives. We go away on vacation for a week or two or more. We enjoy it, but when we come home, we find ourselves saying: It was nice to get away for a spell, but we're really happy to be home again.

Most colleges and universities have each year a few days of homecoming when graduates return to campus to be with those with whom, for a while at least, they saw their school as their "home" away from home. Yet it was home for them only temporarily. After the homecoming week-end they returned to their own home where, ideally at least, they come back to a community of love shared by parents and children. Home is experienced as a place of security and peace—a place where we feel, well, "at home." The family home is not primarily a building; rather—again I am speaking of an ideal—it is a community of people living together, eating together, playing together, crying together and laughing together. Home means sharing with one another. It is a place where others are welcome, where friends and sometimes strangers are offered hospitality.

I read the story recently of a family whose house caught fire and burned to the ground. A family friend said to the fifteen-year-old daughter: "I am so sorry that you lost your home." The youngster replied: "Oh, we haven't lost our home. We have a home. We just don't have a house to put it in."

The late Cardinal Bernardin, who was archbishop of Chicago, won the love and affection of many people by his saintly life and death. On one occasion he went to Italy and visited the area in northern Italy that his parents had come from. Over the years he had looked at many photos of that area in the albums that his mother had kept. When he got to that village, there was so much of it that he recognized at once: the buildings, the hills, the people. His reaction was a joyous one. He said: "My God! I know this place. I am at home!"

It seems to me that this is the kind of remembrance we may well experience when we passed through death's portal into eternal life with God. Heaven will always be a surprise, but at a deep level it will also be in some ways a remembering. We will be struck with the feeling that what we will then be experiencing in eternity is really not alien to what we had already experienced in our earthly home in this mortal life—not alien, to be sure, but far surpassing it in wonderment and delight. Perhaps our joy of recognition will move us to say: "My God! I know this place. At last I am at home!" Heaven is the place Jesus has gone to prepare "home" for us. In death he takes us home to our home that is his "home" with the Father.

This sense of somehow having been there will not surprise us. Despite what I said above about the indescribability of heaven, I do agree with the poet William Wordsworth that there are moments in our lives when we experience "intimations of immortality." In any reflective life, there are certain overwhelming moments when we think of the preciousness of life and ponder where our lives may be leading us. At such times we can easily feel a closeness to the life that awaits all of us, a kind of mysterious bond with another life, another world (or another home, if you will) that may seem remote from us most of the time, but at certain times is preciously close. We have fleeting glimpses of our true home with God. I think of the words of Zosima the Elder in Dostoyevsky's great novel *The Brothers Karamazov*: "Much on earth [he tells us] is concealed from us, but in place of it we have been granted a secret, mysterious sense of our living bonds with the other world, with the higher heavenly world....The roots of our thoughts and feelings are not here but in that other world."

He speaks of the seed God sows in us that is from that other world but can only sprout and come to full bloom in the world from which it came. In other words we have to go to that other world to be fully ourselves. It is only there that we are truly "at home."

Yet when we distinguish this world and that other world, we must be careful not to think that we are talking about geography. That other world does not exist apart from this world, say like another planet might exist in our solar system, apart from planet earth. No, that other world commingles with this world. We can discover it, experience it—even if only partially and ever so incompletely—in this life.

Death is the full discovery of that other world—that was always there but we didn't know it. For that other world is nothing other than the life of God communicated to us—partially in this life, fully in death. We are, after all, created in the image of God. The reality of God is as it were imprinted in us. Or as Wordsworth expressed it, "Trailing clouds of glory do we come / from God who is our home."

Death is finding a place to dwell in that is truly home. We have here no lasting city. We are looking for that city that is to come. Yet the paradox is that we are already in it. But we have to discover that we are there. Our prayers, our deeds, our loves, our joys and sorrows, our failures, our frustrations are all ways in which we are led to make that discovery. Death is the final step in that discovery. Death is not going somewhere. It is finding Someone. For we die into God. We return to God who is our home. And in God we find all. We discover our family, our friends. We find that wonderful family that we call the communion of saints. With them and in God we know that we've come home. What a wonderful homecoming, full of joy and enduring peace—and it lasts forever!

A Family Reunion

One of the joys of coming home is being united once again with family and friends. This may well be the answer to a frequently asked question: "In heaven will I know all those I have known and loved in this life?" Since it is difficult for us to think of coming home if family and friends were not there, it seems that the answer should be: Yes, in heaven you will be united with those whom you loved and cherished in this world. The scenario of a family reunion has been a perennial image of heaven that many people find congenial to their hopes and dreams about eternal life.

Will we know our loved ones in heaven? Saint Cyprian, bishop of Carthage in northern Africa in the third century, writing for his fellow Christians, who lived under the constant threat of death in a time of persecution, encouraged them with the hope that death will be their "going home" to be with their loved ones. He writes:

> Let us greet the day which assigns each of us to his own home.... Why do we not hasten and run, that we may behold our country, that we may greet our parents? There a great number of our dear ones awaiting us, and a dense crowd of parents, brothers, children is longing for us, already assured of their safety, and still longing for our salvation. What gladness there will be for them and for us, when we enter their presence and share their embrace![80]

The New Testament parables about the kingdom of God stress the communal nature of dwelling in heaven. Heaven is presented as a banquet, a wedding feast, a new city. It is not separate individuals who enjoy eternal life, but a redeemed community sharing in God with one another. The eucharistic mystery is a special sign of that community of love that heaven will be. In the four beautiful Eucharistic Prayers for Special Occasions, we pray:

> When our pilgrimage on earth is complete,
> welcome us into your heavenly home
> where we shall dwell with you forever
> There, with Mary, the Virgin Mother of God,

Saint Joseph, the apostles and martyrs
and all the saints,
we shall praise you and give you glory
through Jesus Christ, your Son.

Will They Know Us?

Kindred to the question as to whether we shall know our loved ones in heaven when we join them is the equally fascinating question: "Do they know us now?" Theologian Karl Rahner is clearly of the opinion that they do. He writes:

The great and sad mistake of many people—among them even pious persons—is to imagine that those whom death has taken, leave us. They do not leave us. They remain! Where are they? In darkness? Oh no! It is we who are in darkness. We do not see them, but they see us. Their eyes, radiant with glory, are fixed upon our eyes full of tears. Oh infinite consolation! Though invisible to us, our dead are not absent.

I have often reflected upon the surest comfort for those who mourn. It is this: a firm faith in the real and continual presence of our loved ones; it is the clear and penetrating conviction that death has not destroyed them, nor carried them away. They are not even absent, but living near to us, transfigured; having lost, in their glorious change, no delicacy of their souls, no tenderness of their hearts, nor especial preference in their affection. On the contrary, they have in depth and in fervor of devotion, grown larger a hundredfold. Death is, for the good, a translation into light, into power, into love. Those who on earth were only ordinary Christians become perfect...those who were good become sublime.[81]

Jimmy, seven years old, was very fond of his grandfather. He loved the wonderful stories of which his grandfather seemed to have an endless supply. He delighted in the "man-to-man" talks they shared.

Will our loved ones know us and be concerned about us?

When Grandfather died, he was much distressed. The family told him that Grandfather was in heaven and when Jimmy grew up and got old, he too would go to God and he and Grandfather would have a wonderful reunion. This attempt to reassure him seemed only to upset him all the more. Finally, he explained: "But Grandfather only knew me as a seven-year-old boy. He won't recognize me when I am grown up." It would have been wonderfully helpful for him to know that his grandfather was aware of him and could watch over him as he grew up.

Imagining Heaven: Two Novels

Two recent novels have fictionalized—somewhat—the theological perspective that Rahner proposes, namely that our dear ones who have died are not absent from us. Alice Sebold's novel about heaven, *The Lovely Bones,*[82] begins with Susie Salmon's matter-of-fact account of her rape and murder on a dark night in 1973 and her entrance into heaven. From her perch in heaven she is able to see what is happening to her family and friends as they react to her death. She pays fleeting, ghostlike visits to some of them. Susie's heaven is a heaven that is custom-made to fit each person's desires. In her heaven there are schools but no teachers, peppermint ice cream and all sorts of fashion magazines. Just what a fourteen-year-old girl would want. In time she comes to realize that she is not yet in heaven, but only in a kind of halfway place. Here her guide makes clear to her that to be in heaven she has to be free from her all too obvious attachments to the world she left so abruptly. She is not quite ready for that kind of letting go. She needs to see the "lovely bones" (metaphors for her earthly connections) come together in the wake of a tragedy that affected them all. Gail Caldwell, in her review in the *Boston Globe*, sums up the book:

> "*The Lovely Bones* is tender and quirky, and its charms accrue gradually—it persuades you not in spite of its kookiness, but because of it. If Susie's heaven is hardly an afterlife that will satisfy theologians, it is nonetheless a craftily designed alternative universe for a teenage girl—a place where geraniums bloom in winter and where peppermint ice cream is always in season."

A better, perhaps more insightful, attempt to fictionalize heaven is Mitch Albom's *The Five People You Meet in Heaven*.[83] A modern fable, the story centers on "Eddie," who symbolizes the little people whose lives seem to be one insignificant day after another and who never learn until after death the rich meaning hidden in their lives and relationships. Is Albom hinting perhaps at a divine providence that governs all and ultimately makes sense of all?[84]

Eddie spends most of his life as a maintenance man at Ruby Pier, an amusement park on the shore of a mythical sea. His job is to protect the lives of the park's visitors by making sure that everything is in best repair. He faces trials in life: his father's angry discontent with him, his injury in war, the death of his beloved wife. What meaning could he find in such a seemingly futile life? And on his eighty-third birthday he dies in a tragic accident trying to save a little girl from a falling cart on one of the rides in the amusement park.

It's in heaven that he learns that everything that happened to him finally makes sense. He is told that there are five people he would meet in heaven. Each one was in his life for a reason that he could only discover in heaven. That is what heaven is for: to understand one's life on earth. In heaven he meets the five people—loved ones and strangers—who most affected his life. "This," he is told, "is the greatest gift God can give you: to understand what happened in your life."[85] In heaven "you get to make sense of your yesterdays."[86] "Things that happen before you were born affect you," Eddie is told. He is reminded by his wife Marguerite that when she died her untimely death, he did not lose the one he loved. "Lost love is still love, Eddie.... Life has an end, love doesn't."

The book ends with a kind of apocalyptic scene, in which at Ruby Pier, thousands of people, men and women, fathers and mothers and children fill the boardwalk, the beaches, the rides—all people who were there because of the simple, mundane things Eddie had done in his life, the accidents he prevented, the rides he had kept safe. Then above all this huge gathering he saw a woman, "his wife Marguerite waiting, with her arms extended. He reached for her and he saw her smile and the voices melted into a single word from God: *Home*." It is, I think, not too huge a leap to think that there is here a hint at least of the words of the book of Revelation: "After this I looked, and there was a great multitude that no one could count, from every nation, from all tribes and peoples and languages, standing before the throne and before the Lamb" (7:9).

A Letter From Heaven

Writing about these novels that imagine what heaven is like moves me to stretch my imagination a bit and pretend that I have received a letter from someone whom I love and who is now in heaven. The letter comes from CPS (Celestial Postal Service), the date on the postmark is Eternity and the return address is Heaven.

Dear Bill,

I want everyone, and you especially, to know that it's all true. Yes, Jesus has indeed prepared a place here for me—with God. I'd like to tell you about it, but—as I am sure you realize—human language just isn't capable of handling it. Just know that the experience surpasses all you have ever hoped for or dreamed about. I suppose you expect me to say that I miss you. But I don't. For you see I never left you at all, even though it seems that way to you. I say I haven't left you, because I am not really in some other place: I am in God. But so are you. Thus, we are still together—in God. You don't realize that as fully as I do now. But it is so wonderfully true. And some day you will have that full realization too.

The most important thing I want to tell you is to be mindful of Jesus' command to love one another. That is all that really matters. Faith and hope will yield to knowledge and fulfillment, but love will always remain. That is really what heaven means—being in God and since God is love, being in God means always being in Love. You are already there, but you don't realize it fully, because you only see a mirror reflection of it. But someday you're going to experience Reality Itself. You will experience God in the most wonderful way, as I already do.

Now just a word about the praying you do. It's all right for you to pray for me, if it makes you feel better. But frankly, I would prefer to have you pray with me. Join me in praising God. We are after all one with one another in that wonderful communion of saints. We must pray together that the violence and terrorism in the world may come to an end and that people will be able to live peacefully together. That is really what you pray for, you know, when you pray "Thy kingdom come."

I am waiting for you, waiting for the time when you will know me as I already know you.

With joyful greetings from all your friends in heaven,

Your Dear Friend

In light of Rahner's statement: "Though invisible to us, our dead are not absent" (quoted earlier), what would be your thoughts on the following prayer that I heard recently at a funeral liturgy?

Lord God, Mary Doe has gone from this earthly dwelling and has left behind those who mourn her absence. Grant that, as we grieve for her, we may hold her memory dear and live in the hope of that eternal kingdom where you will bring us together again. We ask this through Christ our Lord. Amen.

Heaven as a Garden of Delight

When I have visited England, I have been struck by the fact that what we in America tend to call our "backyard," people in England call their "garden," and rightly so, for generally you will find there trees and flowers and vegetables growing—often in abundance and beauty. It is generally true, I think, that for the most part people like gardens: both the ones they plant themselves as well as the lovely gardens, large and expansive, that invite visits from tourists. Some years ago I was in Vancouver and visited the Butchart Gardens in nearby Victoria. It is a famous attraction for visitors. One can meander among the fifty-five acres of beautifully trimmed lawns and splendid gardens: from the exquisite sunken garden to the Italian garden, to the Japanese and, finally to the exquisite garden of roses. The glorious colors and exquisite fragrance—especially on a sunny day—make these gardens a place of indescribable beauty. I suspect that many people who see such garden beauty (and there are many who come to see) return home with the determination to give more attention and loving care to their own gardens.

The Garden of Eden

The Bible myth about human origins locates the dwelling place of the first human persons in a garden: sometimes referred to as paradise or Eden. The second chapter of Genesis tells how God created the man from the dust of the ground and breathed into his nostrils the breath of life.

Thus the man (Adam) became a living being. After creating him, God created a garden in Eden and put the man in it. In the garden God planted beautiful trees that delighted the senses and provided plenty of food. Adam was given the responsibility of caring for the garden. Actually not a difficult assignment. There was no need for laborious efforts to water the trees and plants that grew in the garden, since four rivers flowed out of Eden to water them. (Two of those rivers, incidentally, were the Tigris and Euphrates.) God also fashioned in the garden the animals and the birds and allowed the man to name them (a gesture that signaled his authority over them). Finally God created the woman (Eve) from the side of the man. (It is worth noting that Eve was a native of the garden, whereas the man was an immigrant!)

This Genesis myth of the beautiful garden speaks to many people of all eras of history as a kind of perennial symbol for heaven. People generally find a garden a delightful place. As a symbol, then, it can provide a helpful way to understand something of what heaven will be like for people of any age, especially those who like to tend gardens or simply to look at and enjoy them. The agrarian lifestyle of the Middle Ages (in that period of history before the establishment of national states) made the people of that era particularly responsive to the biblical story of the paradisal garden described in Genesis. The pleasant life of Adam and Eve (before the fall) living in a luxuriant garden had a strong appeal to peasants living a miserable life of toil, as each day they labored from sunrise to sunset. Heaven, they believed, would reverse the unhappy kind of life that so many people lived. They would no longer be burdened with onerous labor. People who lived with the constant threat of drought would welcome a garden through which four rivers flowed: with comely trees and fragrant flowers spreading out in all directions from the river banks. The blessed in heaven would hear the sweet songs of birds. Crops would be plentiful, the climate ideal (neither too hot nor too cold, but just right). There would be no thirst or hunger.

Moreover, people, living in a predominantly rural society in which they worked from sunrise to sunset, would find the "rest" associated with the garden an appealing image of heaven. We still retain that imagery in our funeral liturgies, in which we ask that "eternal rest" be the lot of our loved ones as they pass through the portal of death. Thus we pray in the funeral liturgy: "May the angels lead you into paradise. May the martyrs receive you at your coming. May they guide you into the holy city, the heavenly Jerusalem." This liturgical hymn easily moves us from a rural image to describe heaven to an urban one: the holy city, the New Jerusalem.

This need for rest is not just a dream of medieval women and men. It is a need we can all identify with. After a busy, active day, we long for rest. How much more so after a busy, active life? Jesus who knows human life from the inside—because he became one of us—understands that longing. That is why he says to us: "So you're tired. I know the feeling. I have experienced it too. Come to me and I'll see that you get the rest you need." Or as Scripture puts it: "Come to me, / all you that are weary / and I will give you rest" (Matthew 11:28). Thus he does for us partially in this life, but fully only in the next.

The rest we get in this life is always partial and not ultimately refreshing. We get the rest we need. We take up our life and work with joy and hope, yet the peace and the rest that Jesus gives us so often yields once again to the weariness of life and the trials it brings; again we become weary and feel burdened. Again we are tired and seek for rest. Our lives are an ongoing search for rest and the peace it brings in the context of a life that is almost always too busy and too demanding. Restlessness is part of our human existence.

But that restlessness speaks to us of something deep within us. It is a subliminal symbol of our need for God: a need that we can never fully satisfy in this life. Hence no matter how calm and peaceful our lives may seem to be, there is always a restlessness of spirit underneath that we cannot fully understand. All we can know is that it is there. There is nothing in this life significant enough to calm our existential restlessness. No matter how much peace we experience, it is never the fullness of peace that we achieve only in eternity. Short of death, which is our bridge to eternity, the lives of all of us exemplify the confession of Saint Augustine who said: "Our hearts are restless, Lord, until they find their rest in You."

Our prayer that our loved ones who have gone to God may find rest is at the same time a veiled disguise for our hope that we too may some day be delivered from life's perduring restlessness; at the same time it is a prayer for the particular measure of peace and restfulness that even now we can experience as the gift of the risen Jesus to us all, even as we realize that a greater and more wonderful rest awaits us.

The Glorious Royal City

For the early Christians, coming out of a Jewish background, Jerusalem, the holy city, the city of David, served as a metaphor to describe heaven. The book of Revelation pulls out all the stops in its glowing depiction of heaven as the New Jerusalem, the holy city. It is a secure city. It has four great walls with twelve highly adorned gates, where one hears "the sound of harpists playing on their harps, and they sing a new song before the throne" (Revelation 14:2–3). Along with their harps, the elders were holding "golden bowls full of incense, which are the prayers of the saints" (5:8). The walls are built of jasper and are twelve huge pearls. The streets of the city are pure gold, yet transparent as glass (21:21). Water bright as crystal flows through the city. On either side of the river is the tree of life with its twelve kinds of fruit, producing fruit each month. The leaves of the tree are for healing. In this city there will be no darkness, only light. Indeed the Lord God will be the light of the city. In the holy city an angel stood at the altar: "he was given a great quantity of incense to offer with the prayers of all the saints....And the smoke of the incense, with the prayers of the saints, rose before God from the hand of the angel" (8:3–4).

Notice how in this description heaven is described in terms of experiences most pleasing to the senses. The sound of the harp (the most beautiful musical sound known at the time) appeals to the sense of hearing, the aromatic spices to the sense of smell, the new song, sung by the saints and angels, to the sense of hearing. Further, in a land where it was difficult to get water, a city with a beautiful river flowing like a main street through its very middle would present an alluring picture of heavenly bliss. Having crops that never failed—crops that yielded different fruits each month that were there for the plucking—offer insights into a joyful and happy existence.

People who take symbols in an overly literalistic way, often speak disparagingly about the "heavenly city" symbol of heaven. It does not make heaven very appealing to them. As the little girl put it: "Heaven is sort of big and they sit around playing harps. I don't know how to play a harp. But I suppose I'd better start learning that dumb thing pretty soon." Some adults, identifying with the little girl's problem, would express their feelings in this way: "Frankly sitting on pink clouds and plucking harps doesn't strike me as an enjoyable way of even spending a lifetime, let alone an eternity." C.S. Lewis lampoons the shallow thinking embodied in such a lumbering literalism, pointing out that one should not take literally what is obviously intended as symbol and metaphor. Thus he writes:

> There is no need to be worried by facetious people who try to make the Christian hope of "heaven" ridiculous by saying they do not want "to spend eternity playing harps." The answer to such people is that if they cannot understand books written for grown-ups, they should not talk about them. All the scriptural imagery (harps, crowns, gold, etc.) is, of course, a merely symbolic attempt to express the inexpressible. Musical instruments are mentioned because for many people (not all) music is the thing known in the present life which most strongly expresses ecstasy and infinity. Crowns are mentioned to express the fact that those who are united with

God in eternity share His splendor and power and joy. Gold is mentioned to express the timelessness of Heaven (gold does not rust) and the preciousness of it. People who take these symbols literally might well think that when Christ told us to be like doves, He meant that we were to lay eggs.[87]

Are There Animals in Heaven?

In the paradise myth of Genesis, it seems that it is taken for granted that there will be animals in paradise. One of Adam's important tasks was to name the animals, indicating that he had authority over them as well as a certain affinity with them. Moreover, in the Noah story in Genesis, in which only a few humans survived, God painstakingly directs Noah: "Take with you seven pairs of all clean animals, the male and its mate; and a pair of the animals that are not clean, the male and its mate; and seven pairs of the birds of the air also, male and female, to keep their kind alive on the face of the earth" (Genesis 7:2–3). This clearly shows a special concern on God's part for the survival of animals at a time when practically all people living on the earth would be perishing in the flood. Can we infer that this same care and concern for animals would also extend to heaven? I cannot answer this question with certitude. But knowing how fond so many people are of their pet animals, I can hope for their presence as one of the surprises in our heavenly home.

An interesting Scripture passage gives us grounds for thinking that all of creation, not just its human members, await redemption. Thus Paul writes: "We know that the whole creation has been groaning in labor pains until now;

and not only the creation, but we ourselves, who have the first fruits of the Spirit, groan inwardly while we wait for the redemption of our bodies" (Romans 8:22). Jerry L. Walls writes, "If heaven involves truly cosmic redemption, it is natural to believe that the animal kingdom will share in it. Since all things find their *telos*[88] in God, it is not unreasonable to include animals in our hopes and to believe that they will be included, to the degree they are capable, in the fellowship of the redeemed."[89]

The Beatific Vision

Human hope for what comes after death has often been expressed as the desire to see God. In the Hebrew Scriptures having God's face turned toward you was a sign of divine favor and having the face of God turned away from you indicated that you were in God's disfavor. This was a figurative way of expressing one's relationship with God. But actually a person could not see God's face turned toward or away from him or her. For it was a strong belief in the Bible that no one could look upon the face of God and live. In the book of Exodus Moses asks to see God's glory. God responds: "I will make all my goodness pass before you, and will proclaim before you the name 'The LORD';... But...you cannot see my face; for no one shall see me and live" (33:19–20).

The New Testament makes the astounding promise that we shall indeed see the face of God. We shall know God as God is. Thus, in that wonderful hymn about love, Paul writes: "For now we see in a mirror, dimly, but then we will see face to face. Now I know only in part; then I will know fully, even as I have been fully known" (1 Corinthians

13:12). A similar promise is found in the First Letter of John: "Beloved, we are God's children now; what we will be has not yet been revealed. What we do know is this: when he is revealed, we will be like him, for we will see him as he is" (3:2). The book of Revelation describes the new heaven and the new earth: "they will see his face, and his name will be on their foreheads. And there will be no more night; they need no light of lamp or sun, for the Lord God will be their light, and they will reign forever and ever" (22:4–5).

> No man ever saw God and lived.
>
> And yet, I shall not live till I see God;
>
> and when I have seen him, I shall never die.
>
> —John Donne

What does it mean to see God? I am reminded of the little girl who took it upon herself to answer that question. She was sitting at the kitchen table carefully drawing on a large piece of paper. Her mother asked her, "What are you drawing?" She answered, "I am drawing a picture of God." The mother smiled, "But, honey, no one knows what God looks like." In a resolute voice the little artist confidently replied, "They will when I get through." We can admire the earnestness of the little girl in pursuing her "project," but it would be wrong to think that "seeing God" means having a clearer picture or image of God.

"Seeing God" means knowing God as God is. In our mortal life we can only know God through images that are drawn from our own experience. We can use very personal images to describe God. We can speak of God's love and compassion through the image of father or through the image of mother; we can describe God as spouse, as shepherd, as rock and shield. These are all good biblical images. Yet pile up images as we will, we can never attain to a full understanding of who God is. One of the words used over and over in the Bible is the word "great." The psalms never tire of returning again and again to the praise of God's greatness: a greatness that exceeds any human greatness that we can think of or imagine. Thus, for example, Psalm 48 tells us "Great is the LORD and greatly to be praised" (48:1). Psalm 145 uses three variants of the word in one verse: "Great is the LORD, and greatly to be praised; his greatness is unsearchable" (145:3). God's greatness has also been extolled in Christian hymnody. The hymn that comes immediately to mind is "How Great Thou Art."

> When Christ shall come with shout of acclamation
> And take me home, what joy shall fill my heart!
> Then I shall bow in humble adoration
> And there proclaim, my God, how great Thou art![90]

Not long ago a priest-friend of mine told me of a non-liturgical use he had discovered for this hymn: every morning as he shaves, he sees his own image in the mirror and the words spontaneously come to his lips: "How great thou art!" No matter what one may think of my friend's obvious need for a good dose of humility, it is important to understand that his very personalized use of the word "great" has drastically changed the meaning that the word "great" has in the psalms or in the above-mentioned hymn. No one, not even my boastful friend, is "great" as God is great. The word "great" applied to God takes on a radically different meaning from what it means when used of humans. We can truthfully say of God that God is "great" because something of what "greatness" means in humans is in God. At the same time we could just as easily say: "God is not great" because the puny greatness of humans is as nothing compared to the greatness of God. It is not simply that God has a lot more greatness than we have; rather God's greatness absolutely transcends whatever we might call greatness in any human person.

All we can say, then, about our knowledge of God in this mortal phase of our existence is that it is "mediated" knowledge. By this I mean that we see God through the "medium" of images drawn from our earthly experience. To "know God as God is in the divine Self" is to know God "immediately," which is to say, through no medium. It means to know God directly, with nothing intervening between God and us. It is union with God in which we share in God's own knowledge of the divine Self. This is what has been traditionally called the "Beatific Vision." Yet notice how the very term we use to describe what is direct, unmediated knowledge of God is actually an image drawn from our experience, namely the image of seeing. This is the problem we inevitably bump into in trying to talk about God: we have no language that expresses the immediacy of the knowledge of God that belongs to immortal life. In a sense all we can do in the presence of the ineffable mystery of God is to be silent. As Léon Bloy wrote, "When those who love God try to talk about Him, their words are blind lions looking for springs in the desert."[91]

Such unmediated knowledge of God that can be achieved only after death[92] means the experience of total absorption into God. We become fully in God what we have been striving to become all through our lives. We become fully who we are. What does this mean? What feelings, what emotions does this experience evoke? I toyed with two possible terms to describe this heavenly experience: joy or happiness. It seemed to me it would make sense to use both. But I decided that, if I had to choose one or the other (which I really don't have to do), I would choose "joy." Joy of course is happiness, but I think of it as a kind of explosive happiness. It is intense, ecstatic happiness. It means that we become happy and we become it in joy. What do we mean by the joy of heaven? One writer, whose writings one would hardly ever be inclined to describe as ecstatic, is Saint Thomas Aquinas; yet when he writes about the joy of heaven in his *Summa Theologiae*, his tone becomes excited, exhilarating. In fact, he even goes so far as to invent a new Latin word. Thus, he isn't content simply to say that the blessed in heaven are "perfectly full of joy" (*perfecte plenum*); he goes further, insisting that their joy is super-full (*superplenum*). The joy we shall experience in heaven, he would tell us, is not just the regular grade of joy. It's premium joy. Joy beyond our possibility to conceive. Everything that the blessed ever desired is fulfilled when they enter into God.

In proof of this extravagant statement Saint Thomas quotes the familiar words of Saint Paul: "It has not even entered into the human mind what God has prepared for those who love God." In a sense Saint Thomas is going Jesus one better. In his discourse at the Last Supper, Jesus says to his beloved disciples: Your joy will be complete. Thomas says it will be even more than that. It will be joy full measure, joy flowing over and spreading quite beyond our hopes and expectations.

Coming to know God as God actually is means entering into that circulation of love that is the life of the Holy Trinity. We need to be aware of the uniqueness of God's love. Its very essence is to circulate. By that I mean, God's love goes from one divine Self to another without ever finding a Self that blocks or impedes that flow of love. The blessed in heaven are taken into that circulation of love and in it they find their total fulfillment. Saint Bonaventure describes the life of the blessed in heaven in these beautiful words:

> When we do live that life, we shall understand fully, we shall love completely, and our desires will be totally satisfied. Then, with all our needs fulfilled, we shall truly know the love that surpasses understanding and so be filled with the fullness of God.[93]

R.S. Thomas, the Welsh poet, speaks of this entrance into God as being overwhelmed by the reality of God.

> As I had always known
> He would come, unannounced...
> I looked at him, not with the eye
> Only, but with the whole
> of my being, overflowing with
> Him as a chalice would with the sea.[94]

The unheralded character of God's coming to the blessed in heaven is matched only by the completeness with which one is overwhelmed by God's very being, as the chalice we place on our altar would be overwhelmed if it were placed in the sea. Death means being placed in God (like a chalice might be placed in the sea) and being overwhelmed by God's love. Death means being placed in Love.

Being in love with another human being is surely one of the healthiest and happiest experiences that can happen to us in this life. Being in love transforms an ordinary prosaic life suddenly into poetry. It is an experience that brings insights, intuitions, blessings that before one never even realized could exist. Scripture tells us "God is love." Imagine what it must be, not simply to be in love with someone, but to be in Love. Period. We can only be filled with awe.

Questions About the Blessed in Heaven

What Kind of Body Will They Have?

What is a risen body like? Obviously, not having entered as yet into the full experience of risen life, we have no clear answer to such a question. But the Gospel has something to say about the risen body. For it tells us of Jesus' risen body. And his body is very much a body that one can reach out and touch. He invites his disciples to do so. "Touch me and see," Jesus says to them. He even eats a piece of fish in their presence.

All this is to show us that the risen body, though different from the body we now possess, is still, in a mysterious way, our body. Notice how, in all the resurrection stories, the disciples at first fail to recognize Jesus. He is different. He doesn't bother to knock on the door and ask them to open the locks they had put there. No, suddenly, without any door being opened, he was just there. He had never done that before! So clearly he is different. Yet when finally they do recognize him, it is still the bodily Jesus whom they knew before the Resurrection. Though he is different, it is the Jesus they had always known.

What is a risen body like? Jesus' body? The bodies of our parents, our aunts and uncles who have died? Saint Paul tried to help. He speaks of the risen body as a "spiritual body." I take this to mean that it is a body totally subject to spirit, but still very much a material body. But of course Paul had no more experience of a risen body than you or I have.

I want to emphasize, though, that the risen body is truly a body, because Christian teaching about resurrection focuses, not on an immortal soul (the emphasis of Greek philosophy, as I have already mentioned), but on a transfigured world of glorified bodies. In a homily on the Feast of the Ascension, Karl Rahner describes that feast as "a festival of the future of the world." Christians, Rahner suggests, are the most sublime of materialists. For we believe that this matter (Christ's body, our bodies) will last forever. We shall experience eternal life in the fullness of our personhood.

What Will They Look Like?

What will the blessed in heaven look like? Many early Christian writers argued that the "citizens of heaven" would be naked, recreating the situation in paradise. This time, however, nakedness would give rise neither to shame nor to sexual lust, but would simply be accepted as the natural and innocent state of humanity. Others, however, argued that "the inhabitants of the new Jerusalem would be clothed in finery, reflecting their status as citizens of God's chosen city."[95]

How Old Will They Be?

Yet another question that has stirred human curiosity over the centuries concerns the age of the blessed. This was much discussed by medieval theologians. The answer they seem generally to have arrived at was that, no matter what the age of their death, their age in the heavenly city would be that of Jesus and therefore probably thirty or thirty-three. Alister E. McGrath cites a text of Peter Lombard: "A boy who dies immediately after being born will be resurrected in that form that he would have had if he had lived to the age of thirty."[96]

In a whimsical story (that may pose a few theological problems!), Mark Twain finds that the heavenly citizens, while they can be any age they wish, eventually choose to be the age they were used to, namely the age at which they died.

"About how old might you be, Sandy?"

"Seventy-two."

"I judged so. How long have you been in heaven?'

"Twenty-seven years, come Christmas."

How old was you when you come up?"

"Why, seventy-two, of course."

"You can't mean it!"

"Why can't I mean it?"

"Because if you were seventy-two then, you are naturally ninety-nine now."

"No, I ain't. I stay the same age as when I come."

"Well...down below, I always had an idea that in heaven we would all be young and bright and spry."

"Well, you can be young if you want to. You've only got to wish."

"Well, then, why didn't you wish?"

"I did. They all do. You'll try it someday, like enough; but you'll get tired of the change pretty soon."

At this point the heavenly citizen confides that he tried being young, went to parties and picnics and dances, but he soon got bored with it all. He goes on, "What I wanted was early to bed and early to rise, and something to do; and when my work was done I wanted to sit quiet, smoke and think—not tear around with a parcel of giddy young kids." Two weeks of being young, he says, was enough. He went back to seventy-two.[97]

It may well be that this Twain story has a point that goes beyond our reflection on heaven. It speaks to our culture that prizes youth so highly that it has difficulty in imagining that someone who has reached the age of seventy-two could be quite happy to have achieved the wisdom that comes with age and would have no desire to return to a life of care-free youth.

Does Sexuality Exist in Heaven?

A related question: Does our sexuality remain in heaven? There is one passage in the Scriptures that seems, in part at least, to speak to this question. The passage involves a debate between Jesus and the Sadducees (Mark 12:8–27). The Sadducees were a party of Judaism in Jesus' time who denied the Resurrection. They concoct a rather silly story[98] in their attempt to poke fun at the very notion of resurrection. They tell of a woman who, successively, married seven men. The story is an extreme example of the law of the levirate marriage (Deuteronomy 25:5) which required that if a man died without an heir, his brother was obliged to marry the widow. The Sadducees' story is about a woman who by the provisions of this law married seven men. (One must say the last five at least must have been very brave men indeed!) Derisively they ask Jesus: "In the resurrection whose wife will she be?" In reply Jesus says: "Is not this the reason you are wrong, that you know neither the scriptures nor the power of God? For when they rise from the dead, they neither marry nor are given in marriage, but are like angels in heaven" (Mark 12:28). Jesus' reply should not be taken as a description of what afterlife will be, for the point of his words is to make clear that God has the power to bring about a new way of being in communion with God. At most his words seem to suggest that there will be no procreation in heaven. In no way should they be taken to mean that in risen life we shall be asexual beings. Our sexuality, after all, is not something we *have;* it is something we *are.* Sexuality involves mystery: the mystery of human intimacy that in some dim way mirrors the intimacy of God with his creatures. It may well be that one of the surprises that awaits us in heaven is the full revelation of the true meaning of human intimacy. Alvin Plantinga sees our sexual drive *(eros)* as pointing to something deeper than itself:

> Sexual eros with its longings and yearnings is a sign and foreshadowing of the longing and yearning for God that will characterize us in our healed and renewed state in heaven; and sexual satisfaction and union, with its transports of ecstasy, is a sign and foreshadowing of the

deeper reality of union with God—a union that is at present for the most part obscure to us."[99]

"Plantinga's interpretation of eros," as Jerry L. Walls points out, "turns on its head the Freudian view that religious desire is actually sublimated sexual desire."[100]

Who Will Be in Heaven?

You have probably heard the oft-told story of a group of brand-new arrivals in heaven who are taken on a tour. They come upon a place that is surrounded by very high walls. Their guide tells them: "You have to be quiet when you come near this place. It's where the Catholics are, and they think they are the only ones here."

There was a time when the church did indeed teach that "outside the church there is no salvation." This teaching was linked with the faith-affirmation that Jesus Christ is the universal savior. Even as late as the fifteenth century the church taught that explicit faith in Jesus was necessary for salvation. The discovery of the "new world" raised the question of the salvation of the huge numbers of peoples who had never known Christ or would never come to know him. Would they be lost eternally if they were not baptized? This was the question that drove people like Saint Francis Xavier (1506–1551) to go to the East to bring the gospel message to people who had never heard of Christ. He preached tirelessly in India, in Ceylon, in Japan. He was on his way to bring that message to China when he fell ill. From his deathbed he looked longingly toward that huge country—and with a heavy heart. He grieved for all those people who, he firmly believed, would be damned to hell because he was unable to bring baptism to them.

To deal with the problem of the possibility of salvation for those who, through no fault of their own, never heard the gospel, theories developed about salvation through *implicit* faith in Christ—that implicit faith expressed in a person's effort to follow the dictates of conscience. This was understood, however, as applying singly to each particular case. The ordinary way of salvation was still through membership in the church. All others who were saved achieved salvation in an extraordinary way known only to God. Such an approach seemed to lead to the strange anomaly that more people might well be saved in the extraordinary way than in the ordinary way!

The Second Vatican Council, speaking of the duty that Christians have of battling evil and patterning their lives after the death of Jesus as they hasten toward sharing in his Resurrection, says:

> All this holds true not only for Christians, but for all men of good will in whose hearts grace works in an unseen way, and since the ultimate vocation of man is in fact one and divine, we ought to believe that the Holy Spirit in a manner known only to God offers to every man the possibility of being associated with this paschal mystery.[101]

This statement makes clear that the church does indeed teach that salvation outside the church is, by God's hidden grace, a true possibility for people of various religions. The shrinking of the global world means that more and more we experience contact with people of these religions. Such contacts force us to look at some serious questions. Are these people saved in spite of their religions? Or are they saved *because* they are Hindus or Buddhists or another faith? The Second Vatican Council in its document on non-Christian religions helps us to deal with these questions. It says:

> The Catholic Church rejects nothing which is true and holy in these religions. She looks with sincere respect upon those ways of conduct and of life, those rules and teachings which, though differing in many particulars from what she holds and sets forth, nevertheless reflect a ray of that truth which enlightens all people.[102]

To put the issue more precisely, this text forces us to face this question: Do people of these religions achieve salvation individually apart from their religions or do these religions have a positive role to play in the saving plan of God? The more we know about various religions, the more we realize that, despite their differences, all religions deal with common questions: the origin and destiny of humans, the criteria for authentic living, the mystery of suffering, the meaning of death. As millions of peoples find some answers or at least some insights into these fundamental questions from a particular religion that is far removed, historically and geographically, from Christianity, does it not make great sense to believe that God is present and operative in these religions? We cannot restrict God's actions within the horizons familiar to us. God is not just our God. God is God of all peoples. This is not to suggest that all religions are the same. It is rather to say that the God we believe in is a God who wills to save and who uses whatever means of salvation are available to people.

Today it is more important than ever for us to respect the different religions that exist throughout the world. As our world grows smaller and our future becomes more and more intertwined with that of peoples of the world, we need dialogue and mutual commitment to common human goals if we are to survive. As Hans Küng has said: "There will be no peace among the nations without peace among the religions and no peace among the religions without dialogue between the religions."[103]

One thing we can be sure of: In heaven there will be no Catholics, no Protestants, no Jews, no Muslims, no Hindus, no Buddhists. There will only be people: all God's beloved children.

Are There Any Theologians in Heaven?

Death makes us all theologians! For a theologian is one who says a word (*logos*) about God (*theos*), that is, he or she is someone who wants to name God. Yet, try as we will, on this side of the eternal divide, naming God is far beyond our capabilities. There is a book, in the Sufi tradition, which makes this point in a striking way: *The Ninety-Nine Names of God*. The intent of the book is to suggest that there are ninety-nine names of God that we can say, but there is one name that is secret and mysterious. It is a name we cannot say in this life. It is the name that alone describes God and it is a name that God tells us when death ushers us into the fullness of God's presence. In saying that name, the blessed in heaven become theologians *par excellence*.

❧ Selected Bibliography ❧

Bernard, Jan Selliken, and Miriam Schneider. *The True Work of Dying: A Practical and Compassionate Guide to Easing the Dying Process.* New York: Avon Books, 1996. Drawing on their rich experiences of hospice patients, the authors provide a practical guidance for the dying, their families and other caregivers. Bibliography and index.

Byock, Ira, M.D. *Dying Well: Peace and Possibilities at the End of Life.* New York: Riverhead Books, 1998. Dr. Byock, longtime director of a hospice in his hometown, becomes in this book a staunch spokesperson for the hospice movement. In twelve chapters, each telling the moving story of one individual, he concretizes different aspects of the dying process that can make the end of life as meaningful and precious as its beginning. A forty-page appendix, in question and answer form, deals with specific issues that families and friends have to face when a loved one is dying. Brief bibliography and index.

Huntley, Theresa M. *Helping Children Grieve: When Someone They Love Dies.* Revised edition. Minneapolis: Augsburg Fortress, 2002. As a clinical social worker, the author works as a children's loss and grief specialist. Children are bewildered and full of all sorts of questions when someone they love dies. This book shows how children at various ages understand death. It offers practical and helpful ways for caring adults to help children deal with their grief.

Kübler-Ross, Elisabeth. *On Death and Dying.* New York: Macmillan, 1969. A pioneering work that opened up a whole new way of thinking about death and dying. She has also written *To Live Until We Say Goodbye* (New York: Simon and Schuster, 1978).

Kuhl, David, M.D. *What Dying People Want: Practical Wisdom for the End of Life.* New York: Public Affairs, 2002. The author shows what dying people want, from his experience as a physician and from the experiences of people who are dying. He celebrates life, affirming that people who are dying are still living and can be helped to make that living comfortable and free from pain.

McDannell, Colleen, and Bernhard Lang. *Heaven: A History.* Second edition. New Haven, Conn.: Yale University Press, 2001. This work is a history, not really about heaven, but about what Christians choose to think about heaven. Extensive notes, bibliography and index.

McGrath, Alister E. *A Brief History of Heaven.* Oxford: Blackwell, 2003. This book is about the development of the idea of heaven in Western culture and the influence it has brought to the literature of the West. It is not a chronological development of the idea of heaven as in the book of McDannell and Lang; instead it offers a different approach, arranging its material thematically rather than historically. Index and detailed bibliography.

Schwiebert, Pat, and Chuck DeKlyen. *Tear Soup: A Recipe for Healing After Loss.* Portland, Ore.: Grief Watch, 1999. A unique book, with brief text and plentiful illustrations, that affirms the bereaved and educates the unbereaved. There is a simple story line: Grandy has just suffered a great loss in her life and is cooking up her own brand of "tear" soup that blends different ingredients that were part of her own grief process. Her tear soup will help to bring her comfort as she faces the emptiness caused by her loss.

Smith, Douglas C. *Caregiving: Hospice-Proven Techniques for Healing Body and Soul.* New York: Wiley, 1997. The material in this book is organized around "A Patient's Bill of Rights." Filled with inspirational stories, it offers time-tested ways of guaranteeing these rights for patients. Bibliography and index.

Stoddard, Sandol. *The Hospice Movement: A Better Way of Caring for the Dying.* New York: Vintage, 1992. A classic work on hospice care, initiating caregivers, family and friends of the dying into a new understanding of death and dying that brings together the medical, social and spiritual aspects of that process. Bibliography and index.

Walls, Jerry L. *Heaven: The Logic of Eternal Joy.* New York: Oxford University Press, 2002. In recent years heaven has lost much of its appeal to the Christian imagination. This book suggests that the doctrine of heaven needs to be taken seriously. He analyzes the traditional teaching about heaven and shows how it relates to fundamental Christian doctrines, particularly those that concern salvation. Recovery of the hope of heaven can enable humans to dis-cover their own identities. Detailed bibliography.

Zaleski, Carol and Philip. *The Book of Heaven: An Anthology of Writings from Ancient to Modern Times.* New York: Oxford University Press, 2000. A copious anthology, it is a rich source of human longings for an afterlife that pervades various cultures and religions throughout human history. There are seven sections: The Journey, Lands of Bliss, The Vision of God, The Celestial Court, Heavenly Society, Heaven on Earth and New Heaven and New Earth.

Some of the above books have their own specific bibliographies, which you may want to consult.

❧ NOTES ❧

1. In Rowan Williams, et al., *Love's Redeeming Work: The Anglican Quest for Holiness* (New York: Oxford, 2001), p. 117.

2. See part two for a detailed discussion of the hospice movement and the way in which hospice care can relieve pain and bring quality of life and peace to dying persons.

3. This story is a gift to me from Kathy Quinlan from Isaiah House, a home for the dying in Rochester, New York.

4. Vladimir Lossky, *The Mystical Theology of the Eastern Church* (Cambridge: James Clarke and Co., 1957), p. 121.

5. Robert Nowell, *What a Modern Catholic Believes about Death* (Chicago: Thomas More Society, 1972), p. 43.

6. Rossiter Worthington Raymond, cited in Maggie Callanan and Patricia Kelley, *Final Gifts* (New York: Bantam, 1993), p. 247.

7. *Jesus Caritas,* Pere de Foucauld Association, January 1964, p. 13.

8. For further reflection, see part two on bereavement.

9. *"Le morte est belle. Elle seul donne à l'amour son vrai climat."* (Eurydice, act 4).

10. John Milton, *Paradise Lost,* book 5, lines 573–575.

11. *Liturgy of the Hours,* vol. three, p. 1475.

12. I learned later that he had borrowed this analogy from the famous (infamous?) sermon on hell given by Father Arnall in James Joyce's *A Portrait of the Artist as a Young Man,* parts of which will appear later in this book.

13. Joseph Ratzinger, *Introduction to Christianity* (Ft. Collins, Colo.: Ignatius, 1990), p. 271.

14. John Polkinghorne, "How the Resurrection Makes Sense," *The Tablet*, April 4, 1999.

15. John R. Sachs, "Resurrection of the Body," in Richard McBrien, general editor, *Encyclopedia of Catholicism* (New York: HarperCollins, 1995), p. 1111.

16. Committee on the Liturgy, USCCB, "Reflections on the Body, Cremation and Catholic Funeral Rites" (Washington, D.C.: USCCB, 1997), p. 2.

17. "Reflections on the Body, Cremation and Catholic Funeral Rites," 7.

18. St. Augustine, *Confessions*, Loeb Classical Library (Cambridge, Mass.: Harvard University Press, 1988), vol. eleven, p. 55.

19. Canon 1176, 3.

20. It is worth noting that this sentence about human identity and self-consciousness as expressed through the body seems clearly to affirm that our loved ones who have gone to God must be embodied. For we certainly believe in their identity as that of our loved ones.

21. "Reflections on the Body, Cremation and Catholic Funeral Rites."

22. This information comes from the Tiger Fund Web page on the Internet.

23. *Evangelium Vitae*, 86.

24. *Catechism of the Catholic Church*, second edition (Rome: Libreria Editrice Vaticana, 1994, 1997), 2296.

25. Directive #64.

26. Robert Browning, "Rabbi Ben Ezra," in the *Poems and Plays of Robert Browning* (New York: Modern Library, 1934), p. 289.

27. Zalman Schachter-Shalomi and Ronald S. Miller, *From Age-ing to Sage-ing; A Profound Vision of Growing Older* (New York: Warner Books, 1995).

28. Thomas Merton, *Witness to Freedom* (New York: Farrar Straus and Giroux, 1994), p. 193.

29. Teilhard de Chardin, *The Divine Milieu* (London: William Collins and Sons, 1960), pp. 89–90.

30. While we normally think of terminal illness as coming at the end of the aging process, it can also become a reality in the life of a younger person, as the result of a serious accident or an incurable disease.

31. Saint Ignatius of Antioch is an extreme example of one who made this choice. On his way to Rome as a prisoner of the Roman Empire he was being taken to certain martyrdom. On his way he wrote seven letters to various churches, including one to the church in Rome. So ardently did he desire martyrdom that he begged the Romans not to interfere in any way to prevent his being thrown to the wild beasts in the Coliseum. His desire was fulfilled: He died a martyr in AD 107.

32. Richard A. McCormick, *Corrective Vision: Explorations in Moral Theology* (Kansas City, Mo.: Sheed and Ward, 1994), p. 217.

33. Thomas O'Donnell, "Comment," *Medical Moral Newsletter,* February 1987, p. 7.

34. *National Catholic Reporter,* March 26, 2004.

35. See *Origins,* April 8, 2004, p. 4.

36. It should be kept in mind that this statement of the pope appears in a talk he gave at a conference. It does not, therefore, carry the authoritative weight of a more formal document, such as an encyclical.

37. From *Catholic Trends*, Catholic News Service, April 10, 2004.

38. This is my summary of the mission statement on the Web page of St. Joseph's Hospice.

39. Cicely Saunders and Mary Baines, *Living with Dying: The Management of Terminal Illness* (New York: Oxford, 1983), p. vi.

40. Sandol Stoddard, *The Hospice Movement: A Better Way of Caring for the Dying* (New York: Vintage, 1992), p. 90.

41. Jan Selliken Bernard and Miriam Schneider, *The True Work of Dying* (New York: Avon, 1997), pp. 3–4.

42. An unpublished talk delivered at the Chautauqua Institution in Chautauqua, New York, July 8, 1996.

43. The homes caring for the dying are not licensed or certified. They are linked with a local hospice agency and it is through these agencies that they are able to receive Medicare or Medicaid. State law (at least in New York State) limits them to two beds for their residents. (Some prefer to use the name "resident" in place of "patient," since they try to provide a "home" atmosphere for those who come to them.)

44. Stoddard, p. 231.

45. Interestingly, in the Catholic church the "pallium" is the cloak of lamb's wool that the pope gives to archbishops.

46. Information provided by Kathy Quinlan.

47. Ira Byock, *Dying Well: Peace and Possibilities at the End of Life* (New York: Riverhead Books, 1997), pp. 59–60.

48. *Science and Morality*, p. 264.

49. *Science and Morality*, p. 264.

50. Stoddard, p. 238.

51. These stages may also be stages of grieving when relatives and friends come to realize that someone dear to them is dying.

52. Chautauqua talk referred to above (see note 39).

53. Byock, p. 246.

54. Byock, p. 247.

55. Richard A. Kalish, *Death, Grief, and Caring Relationships* (Belmont, Calif.: Brooks, Cole Publishing Company, 1985, 1981), p. 182.

56. Found at Catholic Apologetics, www.geocities.com/Athens/Rhodes/3542/pryother.htm.

57. Thomas Merton, *The Seven Storey Mountain* (New York: Harcourt Brace, 1948), p. 14.

58. Theresa M. Huntley, *Helping Children Grieve: When Someone They Love Dies* (Minneapolis: Augsburg Fortress, 2002), p. 29.

59. Barbara Johnson, *He's Gonna Toot and I'm Gonna Scoot: Waiting for Gabriel's Horn* (Nashville: Word, 1999), pp. 56–57.

60. "Wisdom and Innocence" (19 February 1843) in *Sermons Bearing on Subjects of the Day*, no. 20 (London: Longmans, Green and Company, 1898), p. 307.

61. Barbara Johnson, *He's Gonna Toot and I'm Gonna Scoot*, p. 21.

62. James Joyce, *A Portrait of the Artist as a Young Man* (New York: Bantam, 1992), pp. 113–118.

63. T.S. Eliot, *The Cocktail Party*, act 1, scene 1.

64. Jean Paul Sartre, "No Exit (Huit Clos)," *No Exit and Three Other Plays* (New York: Vintage, 1989).

65. John Shea, *What a Modern Catholic Believes about Sin, Heaven and Hell* (Allen, Tex.: Thomas More, 1977), p. 77.

66. Marie Murphy, *New Images of the Last Things: Karl Rahner on Death and Life After Death* (Mahwah, N.J.: Paulist, 1988), pp. 67–68.

67. Murphy, p. 69.

68. *Salvation and Damnation* (Clergy Book Service, 1977), p. 80.

69. Hans Küng, *Credo: The Apostles' Creed Explained for Today* (New York: Doubleday, 1993), p. 177.

70. Quoted in *Love's Redeeming Work*, pp. 172–173.

71. In the glossary of terms at the end of the *Catechism*, we read this brief summary about purgatory: "a state of final purification after death and before entrance into heaven for those who died in God's friendship, but were only imperfectly purified; a final cleansing of human imperfection before one is able to enter the joy of heaven" (p. 896).

72. John Savant, "The Dead Need Us," *Commonweal*, September 9, 2005.

73. Rowan Williams, *Open to Judgment* (London: Darton Longman & Todd, 1994), p. 177.

74. John Paul II, *Tertio Adveniente*, 9.

75. *Catechism of the Catholic Church*, 1013, p. 264.

76. *Catechism of the Catholic Church*, 1261, p. 321.

77. Not all readers of Dante would agree with this statement.

78. John Paul II, general audience, July 31, 1999.

79. J. Keirn Brennan and Ernest R. Ball, "Little Bit of Heaven." ©1964 Anne Rachel Music, ASCAP/WB Music.

80. Quoted in Alister E. McGrath, *A Brief History of Heaven* (Oxford: Blackwell, 2003), pp. 140–141.

81. Karl Rahner, quoted in "Of Many Things," George M. Anderson, *America*, November 3, 2003.

82. Alice Sebold, *The Lovely Bones* (Boston: Little, Brown, 2002), p. 328.

83. Mitch Albom, *The Five People You Meet in Heaven* (New York: Hyperion, 2003), p. 196.

84. In the epilogue, Albom speaks of the secret of heaven: "that each affects the other, and the other affects the next, and the world is full of stories, but the stories are all one" (p. 196).

85. Albom, p. 35.

86. Albom, p. 92.

87. Quoted in Constance and Daniel Pollock, comp., *Visions of the Afterlife* (Nashville: Word Publishing, 1999), pp. 16–17.

88. A Greek word meaning "end or purpose for being."

89. Jerry L. Walls, *Heaven: The Logic of Eternal Joy* (New York: Oxford University Press, 2002), p. 91.

90. Originally "O Store Gud," by Carl Boberg, translated from the Swedish by Stuart K. Hine, 1899.

91. These words are quoted by Merton opposite the title page in his book of poems called *The Tears of the Blind Lions*.

92. The closest one can come in mortal life to this unmediated experience of God is contemplation. See *Thomas Merton's Paradise Journey*, pp. 14–15 and *passim*.

93. *Roman Breviary*: "Office of Reading," Monday, week four of Ordinary Time.

94. R.S. Thomas, "Suddenly," from *Laboratories of the Spirit* (1975) in *Collected Poems 1945–1990* (London: Dent, 1993), p. 283.

95. McGrath, p. 34.

96. McGrath, p. 38.

97. Mark Twain, *Captain Stormfield's Visit to Heaven,* cited in *Visions of the Afterlife,* pp. 41–42.

98. Their story may have some connection with the story of Sarah in the book of Tobit: "For she had been married to seven husbands and the wicked demon Asmodeus had killed each of them" (3:8).

99. Quoted in Jerry L. Walls, *Heaven: The Logic of Eternal Joy* (New York: Oxford Press, 2002), p. 194.

100. Walls, p. 194.

101. "The Church in the Modern World" (*Gaudium et Spes*), 22.

102. *Nostra Aetate (Non-Christians),* art. 2, par. 4.

103. Hans Küng, *Tracing the Way: Spiritual Dimensions of the World Religions* (New York: Continuum, 2002), p. xv.

❧ Questions For Discussion ❧

Part One: Here

1. Have you given adequate thought to end-of-life issues? What issues remain to be resolved?

2. In what way does your faith color your thoughts of death?

3. It was once a regular admonition to Catholics to be always mindful of your own mortality. How does the certainty of death change how you live your life? Would a deeper awareness of life's fleeting nature enhance your current life or detract from it? How might it affect the way you treat others?

4. Have you or someone you know benefited from organs, tissue or blood donated by others? Have you discussed your decision with family members? If you plan to be a donor, have you filled out the appropriate forms?

5. How have you prepared for dependents who would be left behind in the event of your death—spouse, children, aging parents? (Example: Have you discussed potential guardians for children or caretakers for your parents or spouse?)

6. When have you had to make or be involved in funeral arrangements for someone else? Did you feel up to the task? What might have made it easier?

7. Have you preplanned your funeral, or discussed your preferences with your family? Do your family members know your opinion on cremation vs. burial or your choice of cemetery? Do you have the information you

need to plan for other family members' final arrangements? How can you invite them to discuss their wishes with you?

8. Are you comfortable discussing end-of-life issues with your family? If not, why? What might facilitate a conversation?

9. What new thought or idea do you have after reading Part One?

PART TWO: HERE ON THE WAY TO THERE

1. How do you feel about growing older? What older friends or relatives provide a graceful example of aging?

2. Has your faith deepened with age? Have your doubts become more of an issue in the face of death? What comforts does the church offer those in their last days?

3. Have you discussed health care issues with your family? Do they know the extent of the measures that should be taken to preserve your life? What factors have influenced your decision on these issues?

4. Do you have the proper legal documents in place in the event you cannot communicate your own will? Have you made sure that your agent, attorney or health care proxy understands your wishes?

5. What is your experience of hospice? How and where do you want to live your last days?

6. How have high-profile cases (Terry Schiavo and Karen Quinlan) made you more aware of the many issues posed by serious final illness? How have they made these issues easier to discuss?

7. Who will mourn your passing? How can you extend comfort to them now that will sustain them when you can-

not? How are those who love you affected by your attitude toward death?

8. What new thought or idea do you have after reading Part Two?

PART THREE: THERE

1. What is your vision of heaven? Of hell? Do these concepts of reward and punishment alter your day-to-day conduct?

2. Purgatory is a uniquely Catholic belief. How do you understand purgatory? Does your faith provide adequate answers to your questions about life after death? Do you understand your faith well enough to satisfy your curiosity?

3. How do you think you will experience the afterlife? Will you still be concerned about your loved ones in this life? Will you have all of your questions answered?

4. In what ways do you look forward to passing from this life? In what ways do you dread it? How can you make yourself (and your loved ones) more comfortable with the idea?

5. What has been your experience of the communion of saints? Do you sense the presence or concern of past friends or relations? Do you want your loved ones to remain mindful of you when you have died?

6. How do you want to be remembered? Are you living in a way to make that likely?

7. What new thought or idea do you have after reading Part Three?

⊂⊃ INDEX ⊂⊃